Cambridge Elements ≡

Elements in Politics and Society in Latin America
edited by
Maria Victoria Murillo
Columbia University
Juan Pablo Luna
The Pontifical Catholic University of Chile
Tulia G. Falleti
University of Pennsylvania
Andrew Schrank
Brown University

T0286873

NEO-EXTRACTIVISM IN LATIN AMERICA

Socio-environmental Conflicts, the Territorial Turn, and New Political Narratives

Maristella Svampa
National Council of Scientific and Technical Research, Argentina

CAMBRIDGE
UNIVERSITY PRESS

CAMBRIDGE
UNIVERSITY PRESS

University Printing House, Cambridge CB2 8BS, United Kingdom

One Liberty Plaza, 20th Floor, New York, NY 10006, USA

477 Williamstown Road, Port Melbourne, VIC 3207, Australia

314–321, 3rd Floor, Plot 3, Splendor Forum, Jasola District Centre,
New Delhi – 110025, India

79 Anson Road, #06–04/06, Singapore 079906

Cambridge University Press is part of the University of Cambridge.

It furthers the University's mission by disseminating knowledge in the pursuit of
education, learning, and research at the highest international levels of excellence.

www.cambridge.org
Information on this title: www.cambridge.org/9781108707121
DOI: 10.1017/9781108752589

First published 2019

A catalogue record for this publication is available from the British Library.

ISBN 978-1-108-70712-1 Paperback
ISSN 2515-5245 (print)
ISSN 2515-5253 (online)

Neo-extractivism in Latin America

Socio-environmental Conflicts, the Territorial Turn, and New Political Narratives

Elements in Politics and Society in Latin America

DOI: 10.1017/ 9781108752589
First published online: October 2019

Maristella Svampa
The National University of La Plata

Author for correspondence: Maristella Svampa, maristellasvampa@yahoo.com
and correo@maristellasvampa.net

Abstract: This Element analyzes the political dynamics of neo-extractivism in Latin America. It discusses the critical concepts of neo–extractivism and the commodity consensus and the various phases of socio-environmental conflict, proposing an eco-territorial approach that uncovers the escalation of extractive violence. It also presents horizontal concepts and debates theories that explore the language of Latin American socio-environmental movements, such as *Buen Vivir* and *Derechos de la Naturaleza*. In concluding, it proposes an explanation for the end of the progressive era, analyzing its ambiguities and limitations in the dawn of a new political cycle marked by the strengthening of right-wing governments.

Keywords: neo-extractivism, *Buen Vivir*, eco-territorial turn, Antropocene Anthropocene, commodity boom, progressivism

ISBNs: 9781108707121 (PB), 9781108752589 (OC)
ISSNs: 2515-5245 (print), 2515-5253 (online)

Contents

Introduction

At the start of the twenty-first century, Latin American economies were highly favored given the high international prices of commodities (leading to a commodity boom), which began a period of economic growth. This new conjuncture was preceded by a change in the region, characterized by intense anti-neoliberal mobilizations, leading to the denaturalization of the relationship between globalization and neoliberalism. In political terms, as of 2003, this process was crowned by the emergence of progressive governments (left or center-left, depending on the case) that, above their differences, combined heterodox economic policies with the expansion of social spending and increased consumption. Thus commenced the so-called Latin American progressive cycle, which would spread until 2015.

Likewise, the dynamic of economic growth created a transitional and conflictive situation wherein one of the major factors would be the *commodities consensus,* which expressed the distinction between neo-extractivism and a new version of development. The increased pressure on natural goods, lands, and territories added a dimension of dispute and conflict between, on the one hand, current indigenous organizations, socio-territorial movements, and new socio-environmental groups and, on the other hand, governments and large economic corporations. Indeed, over the years, past all of the ideological differences, all the Latin American governments implemented the return of a *productivist* vision of development and sought to deny or conceal discussions regarding the implications (impacts, consequences, damage) of the extractive export model. Moreover, in the heat of extraordinary profitability, the number of large mining enterprises and the construction of mega-dams multiplied, while the oil and agrarian frontier expanded, the latter through monocultures such as soybeans and African palm.

To denote this phenomenon, a unifying concept was coined: *neo-extractivism*. It is true that this not a completely new development, since the origins of extractivism trace back to the conquest and colonization of Latin America, at the dawn of European capitalism. However, at the beginning of the twenty-first century, the so-called phenomenon of neo-extractivism was acquiring new dimensions, not only objectively – by the number and scale of the projects, the different types of activities, the national and transnational actors involved, and the dimension of the ecological crisis, but also for its political and symbolic aspects. This new phase introduced various dilemmas and gaps within the field of mobilized social organizations and leftist political parties. This demonstrated the limits of existing progressivism, visible in its link with authoritarian and imaginative hegemonic political practices of development.

By 2013, the fall in commodity prices was a far cry from signifying a weakening of this model. Rather, it led to a deepening and exacerbation of neo-extractivism. A process of reprimarization would accompany the advancement of the commodification of economies. This process would not only affect South American countries, but it was also associated with the increasingly prevalent presence of China in the region, which served as both the main partner and the raw material demander.

In this Element, I propose a dialectic synthesis explaining the expansion of neo-extractivism in the Latin American region, especially in South America. I additionally account for the dynamics of socio-environmental conflicts as well as the emergence of new counter-hegemonic narratives associated with the defense of the land and territories. I will argue that above the specific markers (which depend, in large part, on local and national scenarios), the dynamics of the socio-environmental struggles gave rise to what can be called an *eco-territorial turn*. This is illustrated by the convergence of different matrices and the vernacular, that is, by the innovative crossroads between the indigenous-community matrix and autonomic narrative, in an environmentalist key, to which would be added, by the end of the cycle, the feminist key.

Based on this, I first present some of the critical concepts such as *neo-extractivism* and the *commodities consensus*. Then I address the various phases of the socio-environmental conflict. Section 2 presents a summary of the development of extractive violence in the territories. In Section 3, I expand upon some of the topics of the eco-territorial turn, including *Buen Vivir* (BR), the Rights of nature (*Derechos de la Naturaleza*), common goods (*bienes comunes*), and the ethics of care (*etica del cuidado*). I also refer to the debates regarding the development of alternative methods, including post-extractivism, which is a transition and exit from neo-extractivism. The Conclusion proposes the consideration of these issues in terms of the end of the progressive political cycles and its ambiguities and limitations, in light of the opening of a new political cycle, marked by the strengthening of regional rights.

Various Preliminary Conditions

Before moving forward, I would like to provide some preliminary considerations and definitions concerning the theoretical and epistemological assumptions that guide this Element. The first consideration refers to the type of conflict that our societies are experiencing today. We live in complex societies, where the risks and uncertainties caused by industrial dynamics and exponential and unlimited economic growth produce systematic and irreversible damage to ecosystems. This affects and threatens the necessary functions of nature and the reproduction of life. Therefore, the decisions that were previously reserved for experts and specialized bureaucracies have acquired wider social and political recognition. Currently, the supposed models of development, far from being naturalized and accepted without discussion by the population, have raised intense social debates regarding their economic, environmental, socio-sanitary, cultural, and political consequences. Moreover, they tend to provoke political debates.

In this regard, the socio-environmental conflicts that traverse the Latin American region need to be addressed as well. Socio-environmental conflicts include those connected to the access and control of natural assets and territory, which imply divergent interests and values on the part of opposing actors. Concurrently, these actors are involved in the context of a large power asymmetry.[1] This definition leads us to make two clarifications. The first is that debates regarding development have a deep anchoring in the political definitions of a society, and more specifically in its cultural history. Certainly, there is no single development model, but when we reflect on the various models of development present in Latin America, the question is not only epistemological (their conceptual and ideological construction), but it is also political, as a matrix of social objectives.

On the other hand, what has been said does not imply affirming that the entirety of socio-environmental conflicts leads to a dynamic of contestation among the dominant development model (neo-extractivism and its control and domination mechanisms). In other words, not all socio-environmental conflicts demonstrate the eco-territorial turn or are configured as environmental justice movements. The social dynamics are designing different scenarios and gradations, depending on the localities, countries, and social sectors involved, as well as the available imagery and traditions of struggle, including the questioning of megaprojects. In a schematic way, it can be affirmed that there are those social actors who accept the dominant narratives and emphasize the discussion about the distribution of economic benefit; however, there are also those who denounce the dynamics of dispossession and tend to challenge the development model. Yet, both positions can coexist with tension in the same social organization – which is observable in countries such as Peru and Bolivia – with a strong extractive model.

The significance and resonance acquired by those conflicts and struggles that challenge the dominant development model cannot be defined exclusively from a quantitative point of view. The significance of collective action is qualitative in nature; its importance is in terms of generating new trends and new rhetorical value and their impact both within a common field (social movements) and in

---

[1] I follow in part the definition of Fontaine (2003), but I add a reference to the asymmetric character of the struggles.

relation to the society (the introduction of new public problems). One of the hypotheses behind this Element is that the positions can be analyzed in terms of social conflict, insofar as they are integrated in a study of alternative society projects (elite or dominant fractions and subaltern sectors). In this sense, the classic developmental debate on productive, technical, and economic issues aims to be interwoven with another that introduces the analysis of power, by thinking about politics in a context of socio-ecological crisis; through this, it generates the construction of collective imagery about *a desirable society* (Svampa ed. 2014). In this line of thought, where the extractive projects are questioned, the involved populations claim forms of participatory and direct democracy, while they dispute what is meant by "development." More generally, they ask about other ways of building society and inhabiting the world. In short, it is this type of conflict that draws attention today in Latin America, which continually sets new trends, beyond the traditional repertoires and responses, that generate and converge with new counter-hegemonic narratives about territory, nature, culture, and the environment. From this, the goal regarding the design of another *desirable and attainable society* ensues.

The second clarification refers to the scenario of social asymmetry that is constitutive of these conflicts: although the socio-environmental conflicts are also argumentative struggles, they do not operate in a context of equality. It is impossible to deny the effect of lobbying by corporations (mining, oil, agribusiness) on the state and its institutions and on the media, and their interference and pressure on citizen and judicial decisions, even in the electoral processes and the practices of delegative representation. There is a deliberate omission from the political-business sphere regarding providing the conditions for public debate on the consequences of the different forms of neo-extractivism. This aspect is visible in the tendency to obstruct or challenge forms of direct democracy (referenda or public consultations) promoted from social organizations and foreseen by the current institutional arrangements. In contrast, the asymmetry also refers to the opacity of the State at its different levels (national, regional, local), despite its obligation to guarantee citizens the right to access information of public interest. The fact is, when it comes to collecting statistical information on jobs; profitability; investments made by extractive companies; and environmental, social, and economic impacts, much of the information provided by official bodies directly involved – the secretariats and ministries of mining, energy, strategic planning – tends to include unreliable statistics, ostensibly inflated economic projections, or simply replications of the information provided by corporations.[2]

---

[2] An example of this is not only mega-mining, especially in relation to the creation of jobs, but also the exploitation of non-conventional hydrocarbons through fracking, with respect to economic profitability and exploitation projections, among others.

The difficulty of accessing accurate information created one of the pillars that structures the collective debate in the Latin American region. This need to generate reliable sources of information was rapidly construed as a commitment to produce independent critical knowledge regarding the different powers (economic, political, media). Consequently, without ignoring the official data, my work appeals to its own sources (elaborated collectively and in an interdisciplinary way, concerning mega-mining and fracking), as well as to different academic sources (EJAtlas, ECLAC, and research by various colleagues in the region at the national level) and nonacademic (OCMAL-Observatory of Mining Conflicts in Latin America, diverse social organizations, and activist stories) to account for these processes.[3]

Lastly, regarding the place of enunciation, it should be clarified that this Element is not written from a supposed value of neutrality or the distancing of the "experts." To paraphrase Boaventura de Sousa Santos (2003), objectivity is sought but in no way does it advocate for "neutrality," a discourse in which the most varied areas of power have hidden interests. This is a theoretical and methodological approach that is part of the tradition of critical social sciences. This field emphasizes the inequality of environmental costs, the lack of participation, lack of democracy, and environmental racism toward indigenous peoples – in short, gender injustice and ecological debt. It is a theoretical and epistemological commitment that seeks to resume and affirm the critical role that, I believe, academic institutions must play in the social production of knowledge, as well as in the discussion of the issues that run through our society, such as that a valuable dialogue with social organizations can encourage the production of alternative knowledge.

1 Dimensions of Neo-extractivism

1.1 Extractivism and Neo-extractivism

Neo-extractivism is an analytical category born in Latin America that has a great descriptive and explanatory power, as well as a denunciatory aspect and a strong mobilizing power. It would be impossible to synthesize the contributions and characterizations, such the profusion of articles and books produced in the past decade that relate to its applicability to the affected actors and social movements that constitute it. In this first section, I am interested in giving

---

[3] In the case of the mega mining, Machado Araoz, Svampa et al. (*Voices of Alert*, 2011, published in different versions in Argentina, Ecuador, Uruguay, and Peru); for fracking, Bertinat et al. (2014, reissued in 2018); and on development models and neo-extractivism, Svampa and Viale (2014). At the Latin American level, we appeal to the individual and collective contributions of the Permanent Working Group of Alternatives to Development (*EL Grupo de Trabajo Permanente de Alternativas al Dessarrollo*), in addition to academic research at the national level, carried out in collaboration with social organizations, which will be cited appropriately.

an account of some readings that point to the multidimensionality and multiple scales of the phenomenon.

In terms of the "accumulation model," all the authors recognize the historical roots of extractivism. For the Ecuadorian economist Alberto Acosta, "Extractivism is a form of accumulation that began to be massively forged 500 years ago," molded since then by the demands of the metropolitan centers of nascent capitalism (Acosta, 2013:62). In this regard, as the Argentine political scientist Horacio Machado Aráoz affirms, extractivism is not one more phase of capitalism or a problem of underdeveloped economies but constitutes "a structural feature of capitalism as a world-economy ... a historical-geopolitical product of the differentiation – the original hierarchization between colonial territories and imperial metropolises; the ones thought as mere spaces of looting and plundering done for the provisioning of the others" (Machado Aráoz, 2013:131). Furthermore, the Venezuelan sociologist Emiliano Terán Mantovani adds to this argument by claiming that neo-extractivism can be interpreted as a "particular mode of accumulation," especially with respect to Latin American economies, "which can be studied from the social and territorial scope encompassed by the nation-state, without detriment to other scales of territorial analysis" (Terán Mantovani, 2016:255–256).

Other works consider extractivism as a style of development based on the extraction and appropriation of nature, "which feeds a scarcely diversified productive framework and is very dependent on an international suppliers of raw materials" (Gudynas, 2015:13). Thus, for the Uruguayan author, extractivism refers to a "mode of appropriation," rather than a mode of production – that is, "a type of extraction of natural resources" that refers to activities that remove large volumes of unprocessed (or limited) natural resources for export. Throughout history, there have been successive generations of extractivism. The current third- and fourth-generation extractivism is characterized by the intensive use of water, energy, and other resources. Despite the differences between traditional extractivism – which is replicated by the most conservative governments in the region – and progressive neo-extractivism, a new type, whereby the State plays a more active role in capturing surplus and redistribution, thereby guaranteeing a certain level of social legitimacy, the negative social and environmental impacts are incessantly repeated. In addition, the differences between traditional extractivism are replicated by governments (Gudynas, 2009b, 2015).

From my perspective, neo-extractivism is a concept with analytical dimensions. In this regard, contemporary neo-extractivism refers to a way of appropriating nature and a development model based on the over-exploitation of natural goods, largely nonrenewable, characterized by its large scale and its orientation toward export, as well as by the vertiginous expansion of the borders of exploitation to new territories, which were previously considered unproductive or not valued by capital. Consequently, it designates and expands on the activities traditionally considered extractive. These range from open-pit megamining, the expansion of the oil and energy frontier, the construction of large hydroelectric dams, and other infrastructure works – waterways, ports, oceanic passes, and so on – to the expansion of different forms of monocultures or mono-production, the generalization of the agribusiness model (soya, palm leaf, among others) and over-exploitation of fisheries or forest monocultures.

That said, coinciding with the previous definitions, extractivism has a long history with a historical-structural dimension. Certainly, since the time of the conquest (1492), Latin American territories have been subject to destruction and looting. Rich in natural resources, the region was reconfigured again and again in the heat of successive economic cycles, imposed by the dynamics of capital and the international division of labor, through the expansion of the borders of goods. A reconfiguration at a local level would lead to great contrasts between extraordinary profitability and extreme poverty, as well as a great loss of human lives and degradation of territories, converted into zones of sacrifice. The city of Potosí, in Bolivia, marked the birth of a means of appropriation of nature on a large scale and of a mode of accumulation, characterized by the export of raw materials and by a scheme of subordinate insertion in the world economy. Internal specialization and external dependence consolidated what the Venezuelan anthropologist Fernando Coronil (2002) rightly calls *"Sociedades Exportadoras de Naturaleza"* or "nature-exporting societies."

However, the history of extractivism in the region is not linear; it is marked by successive economic cycles, dependent on the demands of the world market, as well as by the processes of affirmation of the national State, especially in the middle of the twentieth century. During that time, national control of extraordinary income occurred, especially in sectors such as mining and oil. The possibility of income capture by the State would also feed a certain social narrative about Latin American nature and its benefits. In the heat of the successive commodities' booms, an *eldoradista* vision appears, expressing the idea that due to the convergence of the abundance of resources or natural riches and opportunities offered by the international markets, it would be possible to achieve development, like that in core countries.

What is the novelty then in this new cycle? Several elements are involved – global, regional, and territorial. For one, the consolidation of neoliberal capitalism translates into a greater expansion of the commodity frontier (Moore, 2011). Certainly, the consumption model associated with advanced capitalism requires a greater amount of raw materials and energy for its maintenance, which promotes the increase of the social metabolism (the set of material and energy flows that occur between nature and society) and brings with it a greater pressure on natural goods and territories.[4] This dynamic of capital introduces the phenomena of recolonization of nature and of dispossession, visible in the process of land grabbing, the destruction of territories, and the displacement of populations. Thus, for example, the pressure and demand of mining resources globally have made companies look for minerals wherever they can be found; in fact, "mining does not respect protected areas, archaeological or sacred sites, human settlements, glaciers, springs of water, headwaters of basins, or fragile ecosystems. Mining has even begun to be exploited under the sea and various samples that have been obtained offshore are analyzed in the hope of finding exploitable materials beyond the land boundaries (Padilla, 2012: 38). After 2002, the mining sector experienced an unprecedented boom in the Latin American region, due to the growing increase in the international price of metals and the liberalization of regulatory frameworks carried out during the 1990s, which granted enormous exemptions to the sector and benefited the large mining companies. According to data from ECLAC, thirteen Latin American countries are ranked among the top fifteen places as global producers of minerals (ECLAC, 2013; OCMAL, 2011)[5].

---

[4] Although the metabolic exchange between human beings and nature is a subject that marginally crosses the writings of Marx, it appears developed by several representatives of critical (and ecological) Marxism in more recent times. While J. Bellamy Foster (2000) speaks of "the metabolic fracture," James O'Connor (2001) calls this process "the second contradiction of capitalism," noting that "there is no single term that has the same theoretical interpretation as the exploitation rate has the first contradiction" (capital/work). Likewise, both highlight capital's appropriation and self-destructive use of the labor force, infrastructure, urban space, nature, and the environment. A complementary reading with the so-called second contradiction of capitalism is offered by the geographer D. Harvey (2004), who places at the center the process of primitive accumulation of capital, analyzed by Marx in Capital, that is, the expropriation and the dispossession of the land from the peasantry, who then throw themselves as proletarians into the labor market. The update of this interpretation, often cited in the Latin American literature, highlights the importance of the dynamic of dispossession in the current stage, which advances on goods, people, and territories. This reading recognizes an important precedent in the work of Rosa Luxemburg, who at the beginning of the twentieth century observed the continuous character of the so-called original primitive accumulation. In Latin American key see the contributions of Víctor Toledo (2013), which associate the study of the metabolic plot with a new socio-ecological theory, and the studies in the key of political ecology, coordinated by Delgado-Ramos, who links the socioeconomic metabolism – "[t]he differentiated use of material inputs, the processing and waste of societies, and the corresponding energy production" – with the recolonization processes of nature (2010: 10).

[5] "If the 1990–2010 period is analyzed, Latin America almost doubled its share of world gold production (from 10.3% to 19.2%), molybdenum (from 15.8% to 31.8%) and copper (from 24.9% to 45.4%). The regional mining production remained stable despite the drop in the price of minerals experienced during 2008–2009." In 2010, Brazil, Chile, Peru, and Mexico were among the main countries of destination, when ten years ago they were only Chile and Peru (OCMAL, 2011: 2–5).

Furthermore, before the depletion of conventional hydrocarbon resources and their easy access, the desire to maintain an energy matrix linked to fossil fuels led to an expansion of the technological frontier. Extracting unconventional fuels, whose economic cost is greater and whose energetic performance is much lower than that of the conventional ones, resulted in serious and burdensome environmental and health impacts. It is in this sense that the United States actively promoted fracking, which not only reconfigured the global energy agenda but also generated a new conflict cartography, which made Latin America – notoriously Brazil, Mexico, Colombia, and Argentina – the beachhead for fracking.

A similar phenomenon occurred involving large infrastructure projects. In the Latin American region, the IIRSA/COSIPLAN infrastructure projects portfolio was signed in 2000. It covers transport (waterways, ports, oceanic corridors, among others), energy (large hydroelectric dams), and communications. Between 2004 and 2014, these plans grew exponentially, from 335 projects to a portfolio of 579 projects (Carpio, 2017: 130). In this context, the fervor caused by mega-dams increased, placing the Latin American region, together with Southeast Asia, at the epicenter of investments. While Brazil is the leader with 256 large dams built or in the planning phase, the trend is expanding to other Latin American countries: of the 412 dams under construction, built, or proposed in 2015 in the Amazon basin, 77 are in Peru, 55 in Ecuador, 14 in Bolivia, 6 in Venezuela, and 2 in Guyana (Vidal, 2017).

Another exacerbated element involves territorial dynamics, which have a tendency to involve intensive occupation of the territory and the hoarding of lands through methods linked to monoculture or single-source (mono) production.[6] For example, in several countries of South America, the expansion of the soybean front led to a reconfiguration of the rural world: "Between 2000 and 2014, soybean plantations in South America expanded by 29 million hectares, comparable to the size of Ecuador. Brazil and Argentina concentrate nearly 90% of regional production, although the fastest expansion has occurred in Uruguay, and Paraguay is the country where soybean occupies the largest area in relation to other crops: 67% of the total agricultural area" (Oxfam, 2016:

---

[6] For Gian Carlo Delgado (2016: 54), "the dispossession of lands should be considered the appropriation of those destined to 1) monocultures, including the so-called 'wild' or emphasize (food/bioenergy/production inputs, for example, corn, cane, African palm), and the production of non-food inputs such as cellulose; 2) access, management and usufruct of resources such as energy and non-energy minerals, as well as 3) drinking water (or blue grabbing); and for 4) the conservation or the so-called green appropriation of lands or green grabbing, which includes from the creation of private protected areas, to the establishment of climate change mitigation projects such as the so-called redd + (projects to reduce emissions for deforestation, degradation, and conservation)."

30). All this redefined the land dispute: according to the Oxfam report (with data from the agricultural censuses of fifteen countries), "As a whole (in the region), 1% of the larger farms concentrated more than half of the agricultural surface. In other words, 1% of farms hold more land than the remaining 99%." Colombia is the most unequal country in the distribution of land, where 0.4 percent of agricultural holdings dominate 68 percent of the country's land. It is followed by Peru, where 77 percent of the farms are in the hands of 1 percent, then Chile (74 percent), Paraguay (71 percent), Bolivia (66 percent), Mexico (56 percent), Brazil (44 percent), and Argentina (36 percent).[7]

The large scale of the ventures serves as a warning regarding the size of the investments, since the mega-enterprises are capital intensive, which indicates the nature of the intervening actors – large transnational corporations – although, of course, national mega-companies are not excluded, such as Petrobras, the Venezuelan PDVSA (Venezuela Oil Company), and even the Argentine YPF (Argentinian Oil Company), among others. Simultaneously, these megaprojects are not labor intensive, given that they generate few direct jobs. For example, in the case of large-scale mining, for every $1 million invested, only between 0.5 and 2 direct jobs are created (Machado Aráoz, Svampa et al., 2011). In Peru, a country par excellence of transnational mega-mining, it occupies barely 2 percent of the EAP (Economically Active Population), against 23 percent of agriculture, 16 percent in commerce, and almost 10 percent in manufacturing (Machado Araoz, Svampa et al., 2013).

Consequently, an increase in social conflict occurred. Throughout Latin America and the geography of South countries, as the number of extractive projects and the territorial areas affected have expanded, the conflicts they cause have continued to grow. An example of this is large-scale mining. The social conflict generated by mining projects is extensive and highly complex to address in exhaustive terms. Each mining project triggers, in and of itself, a conflictual process that begins with exploration activities and does not cease even when it is momentarily stopped, or when the life cycle of the deposit has been exhausted. Given the environmental liabilities left by mining, such conflict persists after the exploitation of the deposit, as can be seen in emblematic cases of Latin American mining in Guanajuato and Zacatecas (Mexico) and Cerro de Pasco, La Oroya, or la Bahía de Ilo (Peru) (H. Machado, Svampa et al., 2012).

Currently, all Latin American countries with mining projects have social conflicts between communities with mining companies and the government. These include Mexico, Guatemala, El Salvador, Honduras, Costa Rica, Panama, Ecuador,

---

[7] Oxfam (2016) data were released in November 2016. These refer to farms and not to people; therefore, landless peasants are not counted and little information about collective property (for the cases of Bolivia, Colombia, and Peru) is provided.

Peru, Colombia, Brazil, Argentina, and Chile. Numerous collective spaces are devoted to the problem of mega-mining, among them the Latin American Observatory of Environmental Conflicts (OLCA), created in 1991, with headquarters in Chile and the Observatory of Mining Conflicts in Latin America (OCMAL), which has been in operation since 1997 and involves more than 40 organizations. Thus, in terms of mining, according to OCMAL, in 2010 there were 120 conflicts that affected 150 communities; in 2012, this increased to 161 conflicts, which included 173 projects and 212 affected communities. In February 2014, the number of conflicts was 198, with 297 affected communities and 207 projects involved. In January 2019, there were 256 conflicts, 5 cross-border, involving 274 projects, 192 cases of criminalization, and 37 inquiries. The countries with the greatest number of conflicts are Peru (39), Mexico (46), Chile (44), Argentina (29), Brazil (26), Bolivia (10), Colombia (16), and Ecuador (8) (OCMAL, 2019).[8]

Another important base is the Atlas of Environmental Justice (EJAtlas), a project in which an international team of experts from twenty-three universities and environmental justice organizations from eighteen countries participate. EJAtlas is coordinated by researchers from the Institute of Science and Technology from the Autonomous University of Barcelona, under the direction of the renowned Catalan economist and ecologist Joan Martínez Alier. EJAtlas is a collective project that includes the participations of civilians. According to EJAtlas, the increase in conflicts began in 1997 and increased especially between 2006 and 2008. OCMAL's database shows an increase during similar dates (Villegas, 2014: 10–11).[9]

Because of this, neo-extractivism serves as an advantageous window to examine the relationship between political regime, citizen participation, and human rights. In keeping with the expansion of territorial and socio-environmental conflicts and their recursive dynamics, both conservative and progressive governments assumed a belligerently developmentalist discourse in defense of neo-extractivism, coupling criminalizing practices and an explicitly proclaimed desire to control the prevailing forms of participation. This behavior has resulted in a rise in State and parastatal violence, visible in the increase in murders of environmental activists in Latin America (Oxfam, 2016).

---

[8] Consulted on January 2, 2019, https://mapa.conflictosmineros.net/ocmal_db-v2/

[9] There is a huge bibliography on mining conflicts at the national level. In the case of Peru, the works of De Echave (2009) and Hoetmer (2013) articulate counter-expert knowledge with a view from social movements. For Bolivia, see the work of CEDIB (2014). For Ecuador, see Sacher and Acosta (2012); for Colombia, the work of Censat (Roa Avendaño and Nava, 2014), as well as César Padilla (2012); for Mexico, see Composto and Navarro (2015) and Navarro (2015), as well as Delgado-Ramos (2010); for Brazil, see Zhouri and Castro (2016) and for Chile, Bolados (2016). For Argentina, see Svampa and Antonelli (2009), Svampa and Viale (2014), Machado Araoz et al. (2011), Machado Araoz (2012, 2013, 2014), and Bottaro and Sola Alvarez (2016).

Furthermore, neo-extractivism is a window through which to read and weigh the scope of the socio-ecological crisis. Certainly, we are witnessing imminent major anthropogenic and sociogenic changes on a planetary scale that have the potential to endanger life on the planet (Anthropocene). Such dangers have been amplified by the current dynamics of development, a product of the burning of fossil fuels, the advance of deforestation, and the loss of biodiversity, among other problems. As a consequence, it is possible to establish a relationship between neo-extractivism (as a dynamic of dominant development) and the Anthropocene (as a diagnosis of the global scope of the socio-ecological crisis), when examining these consequences on a planetary scale.

In short, extractivism covers the long memory of the South American continent; its struggles define a tradition of the appropriation of nature and a pattern of colonial accumulation associated with the birth of modern capitalism. The updating of neo-extractivism in the twenty-first century brings with it new dimensions at different levels: global (the expansion of the commodity frontier, depletion of nonrenewable natural goods, and a socio-ecological crisis of planetary scope), regional. and national (the relationship between the extractive-export model, the nation-state, and the capture of extraordinary income), and territorial (intensive occupation of the territory, land grabbing, eco-territorial turn): in short, leading to policies that are defined by escalating conflicts, emergence of a new politically contestatory grammar, and an increase in State and parastatal violence.

1.2 Commodities Consensus and Developmentalist Illusion

It has been said that in Latin America neo-extractivism expanded in a context of changing times, marked by the questioning of neoliberalism, the emergence of progressive governments, and the boom in the price of commodities. In this framework, we witness the passage of the Washington Consensus, characterized by structural adjustment and the predominance of financial capital, to the *commodities consensus*, based on the large-scale export of primary goods, economic growth, and the expansion of consumption (Svampa, 2015). Indeed, unlike in the 1990s, between 2003 and 2013, Latin American economies were favored by the high international prices for primary products (commodities), reflected in trade balances and fiscal surpluses. Beyond the ideological significance, this time of extraordinary profitability enabled the forceful return of a *productivist* vision of development.[10]

---

[10] The product is based on the idea of indefinite growth and implies a nonrecognition of the limits of the sustainability of the planet.

In terms of its consequences, the commodities consensus was characterized by a complex, vertiginous, and recursive dynamic that must be read from different dimensions. From an economic point of view, it reflected the tendency toward the reprimarization of the economy, visible in the reorientation toward primary extractive activities, with little added value. This reprimarization effect was intensified by the entry of China, a power that would quickly become an important partner for the entire Latin American region. In 2014, in the Mercosur countries, exports of primary goods ranged between 65 percent (Brazil) and 90 percent (Paraguay) (ECLAC 2015). According to Burchhardt (2016: 63), three regional dynamics should be distinguished in the context of expansion of extractive economies in Latin America. First, some countries are defined by their tendency to practice mono-production in the export of raw materials, such as Ecuador and Venezuela (oil), Peru and Chile (mining), and Bolivia (gas). Second, there are countries with a diversified economy that have effectively increased their extractive sectors, such as Brazil, with mining, soybeans, and now oil, through pre-salt oil regions. Third, the countries of Central America and Mexico during the first phase of the commodities consensus did not rely on extractivism but have recently made moves in that direction.[11] In general, the commodities consensus confirmed the Latin American region as an "adaptive economy" in relation to the cycles of accumulation, beyond the political rhetoric of the period, associated with the defense of economic autonomy and national sovereignty. In many cases, "comparative advantages," or the pure subordination to the world geopolitical order, have been used by both progressive and the more conservative governments as a means of accepting the new commodities consensus as "destiny." The role of the exporter of nature has been historically reserved for Latin America; as a result, this has reduced the scope of environmental consequences, the socioeconomic effects (the new frames of dependence and the consolidation of export enclaves), and its political translation (discipline and forms of coercion on the population).

In reality, all governments promote a model of inclusion associated with consumption, since the transitory linkage among state advancement, economic growth, and consumer citizen model was a possible condition for electoral success and permanence in the power of the different governments (by way of reelection). The acceptance of the subordinate position that the region occupies in the global division of labor is one of the core areas that the Washington Consensus and the commodities consensus have in common. Nevertheless, the

---

[11] Even a country like Brazil, which has a diversified economy, suffered what the French economist Pierre Salama (2011) calls "early deindustrialization," due to the inability of governments to counteract the effects of the Dutch disease – that is, the massive exportation of raw materials linked to the exploitation of natural resources.

commodity consensus should be interpreted in terms of both breaks and continuities in relation to the Washington Consensus period: breaks because there are important elements of differentiation with respect to the 1990s associated with the Washington Consensus, whose agenda was based on a policy of adjustments and privatizations, as well as financial valorization, which ended up redefining the State as a meta-regulatory agent. Likewise, neoliberalism operated a kind of political homogenization in the region, marked by the identification or strong closeness with the economic and social prescriptions promoted by the World Bank. In contrast, the commodities consensus placed a massive implementation of export-oriented extractive projects at the center of focus, establishing greater flexibility regarding the role of the State. This was especially true with regard to the possibility of expanding other economic policies (heterodoxy) and an increase in social spending. This allowed for the coexistence of progressive governments, which tended to question the neoliberal consensus, with other governments that continued to operate under a neoliberal conservative political matrix.

Certainly, in the progressive vision, the commodities consensus appears associated with the action of the State, as well as with a bundle of economic and social policies, directed at the most vulnerable sectors, whose base was the appropriation of the extraordinary profit linked to the export of raw materials. In its new context, certain tools and state institutional capacities were recovered. However, the intervention of the State did not guarantee substantive changes. On the contrary, it installed in a space of variable geometry a multifactorial scheme of complexity of civil society, illustrated by social movements, non-governmental organizations (NGOs), and other actors, but in close association with multinational capital, whose weight in Latin American economies is far from receding and continues to increase noticeably. Thus, although the progressive approach has been unorthodox, departing from neoliberalism, for the guiding role of the State, as the argentinian economist Mariano Feliz pointed out, it was far from questioning the hegemony of transnational capital in the peripheral economy (Feliz, 2012: 24–27). This reality placed clear limits on the action of the national State as well as an inexorable threshold to the demand for democratization of collective decisions, coming from the communities and populations affected by the large extractive projects.

In Latin America, a large part of the left-wing parties as well as populist progressivism continued to hold a vision of development in line with productivism and efficiency, minimizing or paying scant attention to capital-nature relations, and to the social struggles associated with this dimension. In this context, especially at the beginning of the progressive cycle, the dynamic of dispossession was a blind, non-conceptualizable point. It was considered a secondary concerns or was simply ignored, given the structural problems of poverty and social exclusion of Latin American societies. Thus, in spite of the fact that in the past decades the Latin American left and populism carried out a process of revalorization of the community-indigenous matrix, many of them (left-wing and populist parties) continue to adhere to a dominant vision of development, closely linked to the hegemonic ideology of progress, based on confidence in the expansion of productive forces and indefinite growth.

Unlike the openly conservative and neoliberal governments, the progressives sought to justify neo-extractivism by affirming that this method generated foreign currency to the State, which was reoriented to the redistribution of income and domestic consumption or to activities with higher value-added content. This discourse, whose real scope should be analyzed case by case, and according to different phases or moments, sought to simplistically oppose the social question (the redistribution and the social policies) with environmental problems (the preservation of common goods and the care of the territory), while leaving out complex and fundamental discussions on development, environmental sustainability, and democracy. In some countries, this discourse was connected to a previous experience of the crisis – that is, with the exclusionary legacy of the 1990s, which produced an increase of inequalities and poverty. For example, the end of "the long neoliberal night," an expression of the former Ecuadorian President Rafael Correa, had a political and economic correlation, linked to the great crisis of the first years of the twenty-first century (which were riddled with unemployment, reduction of opportunities, migration, and political instability). This topic would also appear in a recurrent way in the discourse of Néstor and Cristina Fernández de Kirchner in denoting Argentina as "the normal country," to contrast the economic and social indicators of their respective governments with the neoliberal years (the 1990s, under the neoliberal cycle of C. Menem) and, above all, with those of the great crisis that shook that country in 2001–2002, with the end of the convertibility between the peso and the dollar.

It is also not possible to ignore the fact that the neo-extractivism of the twenty-first century updated social imagery linked to the (historical) abundance of natural resources. Thus, in the framework of a new phase of expansion of the borders of capital, Latin America took up this founding and primitive myth, fortifying a kind of miraculous thought, what is coined the *developmentalist illusion,* which expressed the idea that, thanks to economic opportunities (rising raw material prices and rising demand, mainly from China), it would be possible to quickly shorten the distance with the industrialized countries to achieve that ever-promised and never-realized development of these societies. In the crude language of dispossession (the neoliberal perspective) as in that which aimed at the control of the surplus by the State (progressive perspective), the models of current development, based on extractive paradigm, updated the *eldoradista* imagery (*imaginario eldoradista*) that inter-twines the history of the continent in a contradictory way (Svampa, 2018b).

Consequently, the Latin American scenario was showing not only a link con-necting neo-extractivism, developmentalist illusion, and neoliberalism, paradig-matically expressed by the governments of Peru and Colombia, but also connecting neo-extractivism, developmentalist illusion, and progressive governments, which resulted in the complicated relationship between them and the indigenous and socio-environmental movements. The most paradoxical cases during the peak of the progressive cycle were Bolivia and Ecuador: it was in these two countries, and within the framework of strong participatory processes, that new narratives arose that had the construction of a plurinational state, indigenous autonomies, and the orientation to *Buen Vivir* and the *Derechos de la Naturaleza* as their axes.

In short, the consensus of commodities also has a political-ideological burden, as it alludes to the idea that there would be an agreement, either implicit or explicit, about the irresistible nature of the current neo-extractivist dynamic, a product of the growing global demand for primary goods and energy. We speak of "consensus" as it happened in the golden years of neoliberalism, between the 1980s and 1990s, when neoliberalism appeared as a unique discourse (there was no alternative). From the year 2000, the political elites of the region (whether they be progressive or conservative) would argue that there is no alternative to neo-extractivism, which would end up functioning as a threshold or historical-comprehensive horizon regarding the production of alternatives to neo-extractivism. The consequences included the impossibility of a pluralistic debate and the stigmatization of critical discourses, which would end up being categorized in the fields of anti-modernity and of the denial of progress, if not of "irrationality," "*pachamamismo*," (Pachamama means "nature", so Pachamamism is a pejorative term that refers a romantic or idealistic vision of nature) "child environmentalism," including "colo-nial environmentalism," allegedly driven by NGOs or "foreign agents."

Thus, unlike the 1990s, when the neoliberal model unidirectionally refor-matted the continent, the new century was marked by a set of tensions and contradictions that were difficult to process. From the passage of the Washington Consensus to the consensus of the commodities, new problems and paradoxes were introduced that even reconfigured the horizon of Latin American critical thinking and the entirety of the left.

1.3 New Dependencies and Challenges of Latin American Regionalism

Another element to consider when talking about the neo-extractivism of the twenty-first century is the growing role of China in Latin America. Toward the beginning of the progressive political cycle, too few analysts and politicians envisaged the growing relationship between the countries of the region and China, arguing that it offered the possibility of expanding the margins of regional autonomy, in relation to the traditional US hegemony. Indeed, in an international scenario marked by the transition from a bipolar world to a multipolar one, the relationship with China developed a strategic political sense in the geopolitical equilibriums of the Latin American region. It was the Venezuelan ex-president Hugo Chávez himself who led this type of positioning, carrying out a policy of notorious rapprochement with China, in which he saw a commercial and political ally suitable to enable a degree of separation from the United States.

Circa 2000, China did not hold a relevant position as a destination for exports or origin of imports for the countries of the Latin American region. However, by 2013 it had become the first source of imports for Brazil, Paraguay, and Uruguay; the second in the case of Argentina, Chile, Colombia, Costa Rica, Ecuador, Honduras, Mexico, Panama, Peru, and Venezuela; and the third for Bolivia, Nicaragua, El Salvador, and Guatemala. The exchange is, however, asymmetric. While 84 percent of exports from Latin American countries to China are commodities, 63.4 percent of Chinese exports to the region are manufactured goods. To mention a few cases: Argentina basically exports soybeans, oleaginous fruits, and vegetable oils; Chile, copper; Brazil, soybeans and iron ore; Venezuela and Ecuador, oil; Peru, iron ore and other minerals (Svampa and Slipak, 2018). Likewise, Chinese investments are mainly established in extractive activities (mining, oil, agribusiness, megastores), which reinforces the reprimarization effect that Latin American economies experience under the commodity consensus. In some cases, they (Chinese investments) are oriented toward the tertiary sector to support the primary sectors. This shift implies a threat to the clusters of small and medium-sized enterprises (SMEs), whether due to environmental contamination or the possibility of exporting directly to China products that were processed previously by local SMEs.

Another relevant issue is loans. Recent studies (Svampa and Slipak, 2018) show that the majority of Chinese loans in the region have been for infrastructure (55 percent), followed by energy (27 percent) and mining (13 percent). The main lender is the Development Bank of China, having granted about 71 percent of the loans to the region, whose main beneficiary was Venezuela, with slightly more than half of the funds lent to finance thirteen projects. Brazil and Argentina also stand out as beneficiaries of the loans, each receiving about 14 percent of the loans made in the region. Chinese loans to Ecuador and Venezuela are taking the place of sovereign debt markets and are guaranteed with oil or some raw material (loans conditioned by commodities), which includes an investment policy with the participation of Chinese companies.[12]

In short, at the beginning of the millennium, for those who were optimistic, the new commercial linkage granted the possibility of a South–South collaboration between "developing" countries in Latin America and China, which was experiencing a meteoric rise; in addition, the realpolitik of relations with Latin American countries would be far from illustrating this hypothesis. Thus, what is the most notorious from this scenario is not the linkage of the Latin American region – inevitable and necessary, of course – with China, but the way in which it has been operating – through the massive export of commodities and the accentuation of unequal exchange. All this was enhancing neo-extractivism and the reprimarization effect in Latin American economies.

The emergence of a new dialectic of dependence also appears associated with the failure of Latin American regionalism. It must be remembered that one of the most important milestones of the new regionalism was the Mar del Plata Summit (Argentina, 2005), where the possibility of the formation of the Latin American Free Trade Alliance (FTAA), promoted by the United States, was buried. Instead, emerging progressive governments created the Bolivarian Alternative for the Americas (ALBA), under the impetus of Hugo Chávez. In a move to support "Latin Americanists," ambitious projects were planned, such as the creation of a single currency (Sucre – the new currency planned by Unasur, which never came into existence) and the Bank of the South, which, however, did not prosper, in part due to the lack of enthusiasm on the part of Brazil. Although Luiz Inaácio "Lula" da Silva later became a promoter of Latin American regionalism, as a semiperipheral "emergent power," Brazil began to play in other global leagues, especially through the BRICS.[13]

The creation of the Union of South American Nations (UNASUR) in 2007, and subsequently of the Community of Latin American and Caribbean States (CELAC) in 2010, initially as forums to process conflicts in the region, outside of Washington, marked the regional integration process. However, all this new institutional scaffolding was far from preventing the United States from signing free trade agreements (FTAs) bilaterally with several Latin American countries

---

[12] In 2017, Venezuela sent 330,000 barrels to China, due to the drop in production, according to Washington's Center for Strategic and International Studies (CSIS) (Svampa and Slipak, 2018).

[13] Goldman Sachs coined the term "BRIC" in 2001, to refer to those emerging economies that would mark the economic and political future of the twenty-first century. BRICS held its first meeting in 2006, with the presence of Brazil, Russia, India, and China. As of 2010, South Africa was invited to join the group.

and in 2011 creating a new regional bloc, the Pacific Alliance, with the participation of countries including Chile, Colombia, Peru, and Mexico. Collective agreements and unilateral agreements were also signed with China (many of which involved several countries for decades). Rather than encouraging the strengthening of Latin American integration, such agreements did nothing but enhance competition among countries as commodity exporters.

Consequently, while it is true that the emergence and rapid consolidation of the influence of the People's Republic of China in Latin America were seen as opportunities to achieve greater autonomy in relation to the United States, they actually led to more unilateral negotiations with China and increased pro–Latin Americanism rhetoric. In short, these ventures promoted intraregional competition and the increase of exports of raw materials but also resulted in consolidating the asymmetries, which comprised a trend for the twenty-first century that deepened the dependency on neo-extractivism.

2 Phases of Neo-extractivism, Social Organizations, and Socio-environmental Conflicts

2.1 Phases of Neo-extractivism

One of the consequences of the current neo-extractivist juncture has been the explosion of socio-environmental conflicts, visible in the empowerment of the ancestral struggles for the land carried out by indigenous and peasant movements, as well as in the emergence of new forms of mobilization and citizen participation, focused on the defense of the commons, biodiversity, and the environment. Given its characteristics (social fragmentation, displacements of other forms of economy, verticality of decisions, strong impact on ecosystems), rather than its consequences, conflict can be seen as inherent to neo-extractivism, even if this does not translate into all cases due to the emergence of explicit social resistance. Over the years, and in the heat of new forms of expansion of the capital frontier, with conflicts multiplied, such social resistance became more active and organized. Based on this, I propose to distinguish three phases of neo-extractivism, linked to conflict.

The first phase, an optimistic one, developed between 2003 and 2008. Certainly, at the beginning of the *new era*, in the heat of the commodity price boom, the extractivist turn was interpreted in terms of comparative advantages, as a "new developmentalism," rather than by the differences between progressive and conservative governments. I highlight the fact that it was an optimistic phase, because the increase in social spending and its impact on poverty reduction as well as the growing role of the State and the broadening of the participation of the population generated great political expectations in society.

Let's not forget that between 2002 and 2011, poverty in the region fell from 44 percent to 31.4 percent, while extreme poverty fell from 19.4 percent to 12.3 percent (Observatorio de igualdad de género de América Latina y el Caribe, 2013: 49). Most countries expanded with an array of conditional transfer programs (bonds or social plans) that would reach 19 percent of the population (ECLAC, 2013), about 120 million people.

In some countries, this first phase was characterized by the expansion of the borders of the law, visible in the constitutionalizing of new rights (individual and collective). The State-run narrative coexisted, with its articulations and tensions, with the indigenous and ecologist narratives. This is exemplified in Bolivia and Ecuador, beyond the growing hegemony of the State-populist matrix and its articulation with the new national political leaderships. This period of economic boom, of reformulation of the role of the State, is also an opaque period. Nonrecognition of the conflicts, which became associated with extractive dynamics, continued approximately until 2008, a period of time from which some governments renewed their presidential terms.

The second phase corresponds to the proliferation of megaprojects, as well as an increase in social resistance. The former is reflected in the national development plans submitted by various governments that demonstrated a clear intention to increase extractive activities. Depending on the specialization of the country, the extraction would be of minerals, petroleum, construction of hydroelectric power plants, and/or the expansion of transgenic crops. In the case of Brazil, the extraction followed the Growth Acceleration Plan (PAC), launched in 2007, which proposed the construction of a large number of dams in the Amazon, in addition to the realization of energy megaprojects linked to the exploitation of oil and gas. In Bolivia, it was the promise of the Great Industrial Leap, based on projects for the extraction of gas, lithium, and iron and the expansion of agribusiness, among others. In Ecuador, it was the beginning of open-pit mega-mining, as well as the expansion of the oil frontier; in Colombia, as of 2010, a set of extractive projects was launched under the slogan "the energetic-mining locomotive." Venezuela had its strategic plan for oil production, which involved an advance of the exploitation frontier in the Orinoco belt; in Argentina, the 2010–2020 Agrifood Strategic Plan promised an increase of 60 percent in grain production, to which was added (2012) the commitment to the exploitation of unconventional hydrocarbons through fracking.

The desire to increase the number of megaprojects was also expressed through the Initiative for the Integration of Regional Infrastructure in South America (IIRSA), later called COSIPLAN, which has already been cited. The main objective of the several Latin American governments that agreed to this program in 2000 was to facilitate the extraction and export of these products to their ports of destination. As of 2007, IIRSA came under the purview of UNASUR, renamed COSIPLAN, which led to an intensification of regional trade and investment of the National Bank for Economic Development (BND) in infrastructure works. However, in various regions, the IIRSA/COSIPLAN projects were questioned and resisted: despite the Latin Americanist discourse that stressed the need to "weave new relationships between peoples and state communities," the so-called infrastructure integration of the IIRSA had clear market objectives. There are 544 projects totaling an estimated investment of $130,000 million. For 2014, a total of 32.3 percent of the investments within IIRSA was reserved for the energy area, concentrated mainly in hydroelectric power plants, which are highly scrutinized for their social and environmental effects, especially in the already fragile zone of the Brazilian and Bolivian Amazon (Carpio, 2017: 130). Moreover, of thirty-one COSIPLAN priority projects, fourteen are situated in the Amazon (Porto Goncálves, 2017: 150–159).

This second stage embeds us in a period of open conflict in extractive territories. Indeed, numerous socio-environmental and territorial conflicts emerged from the local encapsulation and acquired national visibility: the project to build a road that crosses the Tipnis (Bolivia), the construction of the mega-dam of Belo Monte (Brazil), the pueblada de Famatina (Uprising, Insurrection. Famatina is a small village in the province of La Rioja, Argentina) and other resistances against mega-mining (Argentina, 2012), until the final suspension of the Yasuni Proposal (Ecuador, 2013). Alongside these highly visible conflicts that occurred in countries with progressive governments, we must add those that occurred involving a neoliberal or conservative influence, such as the Conga mining project in Peru, which has now been suspended; the mining megaproject La Colosa, in the department of Tolima, in Colombia, finally suspended in 2017; and that of the Agua Zarca dam, in Honduras, suspended as a result of the action of the Civic Council of Popular and Indigenous Organizations of Honduras (COPINH), founded by Berta Cáceres, who was murdered in 2016.

The truth is that in the fervor of the different territorial and environmental conflicts and their recursive dynamics, the Latin American governments ended up taking on a belligerently developmentalist discourse in defense of neo-extractivism. This correspondence between discourse and practice, which occurred even in countries such as Ecuador and Bolivia that had the highest political expectation of change and involved promises of *Buen Vivir* and that emphasized the care of nature and the role of indigenous peoples, illustrates the evolution of progressive governments toward models of more traditional domination (in many cases, linked to the classic populist or national-state model). It also demonstrates the forced recognition of a new phase of retraction of the borders of democracy, visible in the intolerance toward dissidence and the criminalization of resistance. Thus, the various governments opted for the nationalist language and a drift toward a conspiratorial dialogue, denying the legitimacy of the claims made against them and attributing it to "child environmentalism" (Ecuador), to the actions of foreign NGOs (Brazil), or to "colonial environmentalism" (Bolivia).

Finally, in line with the second phase, from 2013 to the present, we are witnessing an exacerbated phase of neo-extractivism. One of the relevant elements that explains this type of aggravated continuity refers to the fall in the prices of raw materials, which prompted Latin American governments to exponentially increase the number of extractive projects through the expansion of "the boundaries of commodities"(Moore, 2011; Terán Mantovani, 2016; Svampa, 2018b). Because of this, not only were the majority of Latin American governments unprepared for the fall in commodity prices – as can be seen dramatically in Venezuela – but consequences would also quickly arise with the tendency to increase the trade deficit (Martinez Allier, 2015) and the recession (Peters, 2016). Alongside this was the decline of the progressive/populist hegemony and the end of the progressive cycle, a fact that will have a strong impact on the reconfiguration of the regional political map, a subject that will be discussed in the conclusion.

This stage of exacerbation corresponds to the expansion of *extreme energies.* Bear in mind that the expansion of the technological frontier allowed us to look for other forms of hydrocarbon deposits that were considered "unconventional," technically more difficult to extract, economically more expensive, and with greater risks of contamination. Following the definition of Tatiana Roa Avendaño of Censat-Agua Viva of Colombia and Hernan Scandizzo of the Observatorio Petrolero Sur of Argentina, the concept of "extreme energies" refers "not only to the characteristics of hydrocarbons, but also to a context in which the exploitation of gas, crude oil and coal entails ever greater geological, environmental, labor and social risks; in addition to a high accident rate compared with traditional farms or conventional calls" (2017).

To go into further detail, extreme energies entail high economic costs as well as burdensome environmental and socio-health impacts. Some of these energies require extraction by hydraulic fracturing or fracking, an experimental technique by which it is possible to extract gas or oil trapped in rocks from immemorial epochs. This technique involves an injection at high pressures of water, sand, and chemical products to rock formations that are rich in hydrocarbons to increase the permeability and, with this, ease of extraction.

There are different discoverable types among the extreme energies:

a) Shale gas, which exists in shale deposits, mother rocks or generating rock formed from deposits of silt, clay, and organic matter, at a depth between

1,000 and 5,000 m (0.6 and 3.1 miles). Shale is a porous sedimentary rock that has little permeability, because its pores are very small and are not well distributed.

b) Tight gas or gas of compact sands, trapped in a more compact geological formation, such as a sandstone or limestone formation.

c) Coal mantle gas, which appears bound to stone coal at a depth between 500 and 2,000 m (0.3 and 1.2 miles).

d) Heavy crudes or tar sands, whose environmental costs are also burdensome; currently being extracted in Canada (Alberta) and in the Orinoco belt (Venezuela).

e) Offshore deposits in the sea, increasingly distant from the coast, in deep waters, which are extracted, in some cases, after crossing thick layers of salt. The depth, as with the pre-salt layer in Brazil or the distance between the surface of the sea and the reservoirs of oil, can reach more than 7,000 meters (4.3 miles).

In 2010, the US Department of State launched a Global Shale Gas Initiative (GSGI, known as the Non-conventional Gas Technical Commitment Program) focused on hydraulic fracturing. In April 2011, the EIA (Energy Information Administration) published a report assessing and locating the main world reserves. Although this study would later be questioned regarding the gas over-estimations that it presented, it is still used as the basis of an argument to defend the possibilities of accessing these reserves. In this study, the areas with the largest deposits are highlighted, among which China, the United States, Argentina, Mexico, South Africa, Australia, Canada, Libya, Algeria, and Brazil stand out. While China and the United States are leading in their use of unconventional gas, with 19.3 percent and 13 percent, respectively, Argentina and Mexico are in third and fourth place, with 11.7 percent and 10.3 percent, respectively.

Argentina serves as the head of the fracking beach in the Latin American region. In 2012, in a context of increasing energy shortages, more than promising estimates of the existence of unconventional hydrocarbons prompted the government of Cristina Fernández de Kirchner to partially expropriate YPF, which was then in the hands of Spain's Repsol. The unconventional hydrocarbons were found mainly in northern Patagonia, in the Neuquén basin, which covers a total of some 120,000 km^2 (46,332 m^2). Beyond the immediate crisis, in Argentina an *eldoradista* frenzy soon broke out, a fact that helped suppress any debate on the environmental and social risks of fracking. This was strengthened by the nationalist rhetoric of the Kirchner government, which claimed to promote the transformation from the "commodity" paradigm to that of "strategic resources," based on State control of hydrocarbons.

Similar to what happened with soybeans, Argentina became an open-air laboratory in its implementation of one of the most controversial hydrocarbon extraction techniques at a global level. A regulatory framework that increasingly favored foreign investment protected this. In particular, the signing of the agreement between YPF and Chevron (2013) served as a gateway for large-scale fracking in the country, which was followed by other agreements of association with other transnational companies. Once again, the consensus of commodities, which projected Neuquén as the new Saudi Arabia especially thanks to Vaca Muerta (the largest shale formation in Argentina), was unique in that the resistant black thread served as a means of formulating a common vision of development to progressives, conservatives, and neoliberals. However, in 2014, while the drop in international oil prices placed a brake on the *eldoradista* frenzy in Vaca Muerta, it did not prevent the beginning of a process of social and territorial reconfiguration, based in Añelo, a small town occupied by the big transnational operators. First, the Kirchner government began to subsidize the production of unconventional hydrocarbons, a move that magnified the management of Mauricio Macri, who also, in January 2017, relaunched Vaca Muerta, in its neoliberal *eldoradista* version, signing agreements that guaranteed labor flexibility and the transfer of the cost accumulation to the weakest sectors of the chain, that is, workers and consumers.

It should be noted that the Vaca Muerta region is far from being the "empty territory" that it was perceived to be by the provincial and national authorities. Around twenty indigenous communities are dispersedly settled. In 2014, as a result of the protests carried out by the Mapuche Confederation (the Mapuche are the most important indigenous people in South Argentina), the government of Neuquén had to officially recognize the community of Campo Maripe, which had been established in the area since 1927. Vaca Muerta is not the only territory in which fracking occurs in Argentina. Fracking is also done in the Alto Negro River Valley area and in the town of Allen, where tight gas exploitation advances on pear and apple plantations and threatens to displace this regional economy. Finally, there is a notable increase in the rate of accidents at work – twenty-six deaths between 2011 and 2018 due to this environmental obtrusion (leakage of gas, explosion of fracking wells, generation of huge oil dumps that do not comply with any environmental regulation, multiplication of small earthquakes, among others).[14]

With similar arguments to those of the Argentinian government, as of 2013 in Mexico, the Peña Nieto government proposed an energy reform that included

---

[14] See Opsur (2019): "There are already 5 deaths produced in 2018, the highest figure in eight years, and 26 since 2011 in the entire country. The majority of cases occur in the Neuquen Basin."

signing contracts with private investment companies while placing the issue of exploitation on the agenda. From this, an emphasis was placed on the exploitation of extreme energies in shale deposits and compact sands, coupled with the objective of being able to manage the fall of oil production and the growing imports of natural gas. Due to public resistance, President Andrés López Obrador, who took office in December 2018, promised to prohibit fracking, but it finally was not forbidden.

In Colombia, in mid-2017, the Ministry of the Environment prepared a regulation that would allow the start of offshore exploitation in the country. For a time, the government did not announce a unanimous position regarding fracking; as a result, important sectors proposed a moratorium. The Colombian Alliance Against Fracking (*La Alianza Colombiana Contra el Fracking*) maintains that if the government decides to continue the practice, fracking will place a risk on several strategic ecosystems, such as the Páramo de Sumapaz (the agricultural pantry of the capital that is considered the largest of its kind globally), the Páramo de Chingaza (whose system supplies around 80 percent of Bogotá's drinking water), as well as other ecosystems. Finally, in 2019, the controversy was resolved in favor of fracking.

Meanwhile, in Brazil, in keeping with the energy reform carried out between 2016 and 2017, the government of Michel Temer promoted investment in the exploration and production of hydrocarbons. As in other countries, this reform opened the possibility that the State-run company Petrobrás would be part of all the oil consortiums involved in the exploration and exploitation of the pre-salt layer, that is, deep-sea oil. This change reversed the 2010 reforms that obliged the national oil company to acquire at least 30 percent of the hydrocarbon fields in this oil region (Pulso Energético, 2017). In 2017, Minister of Mines and Energy Fernando Coelho Filho declared that Brazil would again experience a moment of "euphoria" with the exploitation of the pre-salt layer in the coming years that paralleled the one observed during the administration of former President Luiz Inacio Lula da Silva with the discovery of large offshore reserves.

The rise of fracking has incited wide-ranging reactions within local communities throughout the continent. Citizen assemblies, indigenous and peasant communities, environmental NGOs, networks of intellectuals and academics, and various unions are at the epicenter of this resistance. In Argentina, since 2013 numerous assemblies and citizen networks have been created to promote the moratorium and/or prohibition of the exploitation of non-conventional hydrocarbons through hydraulic fracturing (fracking). At the end of 2017, two provinces (Entre Ríos and Santa Fe) and some 50 municipalities had local ordinances prohibiting fracking. In Brazil, in 2016, some 72 cities prohibited fracking, (Observatorio Petrolero sur. 2018) although other data (Opsur 2018) indicated that 200 fracking-free municipalities exist and several states are considering a total ban. At the regional level, the Latin American Alliance against Fracking (La *Alianza Latinoamericana Contra el Fracking*) was created as a network of organizations that sought to promote debate, analyze the energy context of each country, and dissect the public policies that are implemented to promote and regulate fracking. The alliance also investigates the territorial, socio-health, environmental, and economic impacts caused by this technique and promotes advocacy, mobilization, and resistance strategies undertaken by each country.

Until December 2018, only Uruguay had approved a moratorium on fracking for four years. This was the result of a march held in August 2017, where different environmental groups from Uruguay, Argentina, and Brazil demonstrated against fracking, raising as a flag the protection of the Guarani aquifer, one of the largest freshwater reserves on the planet. The draft moratorium was converted into law at the end of 2017.

The third phase of exacerbation saw the development of new criminal territorialities (*territorialidades criminals*) – the emergence of gangs – a phenomenon that is noted in certain marginal regions of Venezuela, Peru, and Colombia, linked to artisanal and illegal mining. It is located in Peru in the area of Madre de Dios, where there is illegal extraction of gold. In 2016, the criminal organizations of that country had greater profitability than the drug trafficking networks: "They earned 2.6 billion dollars for the production and sale of gold obtained illegally; while the networks dedicated to drug trafficking had a profit of 500 million to one billion dollars."[15] But one of the most extreme cases is in Venezuela. What is now known as the mining pranes or *pranato*[16] reveals the outline of the new territorial extractive, violent and mafia-like, which has as a counterpart a State with little capacity for regulation and territorial control that develops an association with the armed gangs. Although the 2016 massacre in Tumeremo, in the State of Bolívar, was tragically marked by the death of twenty-eight miners and was not the first incident of its kind, it helped make evident the growing relationship between artisanal and illegal mining, rent seeking, and crime, a phenomenon that has been accentuated in the past ten years (Romero and Ruiz, 2018). Thus, we are faced with the emergence of a parastatal sphere, from inside, that involves a large number of legal and illegal economic actors and social subjects. These criminal structures not only control territories but also the population and

---

[15] Accessed on March 8, 2018. http://larepublica.pe/sociedad/1035115-mineria-ilegal-genero-mas-ganancias-que-el-narcotrafico

[16] Strictly speaking, *Pran* in prison jargon means "chief." It is usually attributed to the "title" of "prisoner serial killer born."

subjects, which deals a severe blow for any attempt to reconstruct a democratic project.

Likewise, another phenomenon that accompanies the expansion of illegal mining is human trafficking. In the Puno region in Bolivia, thousands of cases of trafficked women and sexual exploitation have been reported as well as in the Amazon region of Madre de Dios, Peru, where there is also illegal extraction of gold. As affirmed by Livia Wagner, author of the report *Organized Crime and Illegal Mining in Latin America*, "There is a strong link between illegal mining and sexual exploitation; whenever there are large migrations of men to an area, there is a great demand for sexual services that often generates sex trafficking" (BBB Mundo, 2016). In the case of Argentina, trafficking and prostitution follow the path of the oil and mining route, as well as the soy route. The reality is that where socio-territorial configurations are consolidated, characterized by masculinization, disarticulation of the social fabric, inequality and accelerated over-appropriation, there is a reinforcement of the patriarchal matrix, which aggravates the chains of violence. This is expressed in a generation of new figureheads, linked to sexual slavery.

2.1 Territorial Tensions, Dominant Models, and Indigenous Peoples

Currently, there seems to be an implicit consensus among Latin American analysts that one of the constituent dimensions of social resistance against extractivism is the defense of territory and territoriality. Certainly, territory and territoriality are disputed concepts, since they not only appear in the narrative of indigenous organizations and socio-environmental movements but also in the discourse of corporations, planners, and public policy designers. In short, the notion of territory became a type of "total social concept," from which it is possible to anticipate the positioning of the different actors in conflict and, even more, to analyze the resulting social and political dynamics.

In general terms, both in urban and rural movements, the territory serves as a space of resistance and also, progressively, as a place of reappropriation and creation of new social relations. From the perspective of social movements, territoriality as a "material dimension" has often been understood exclusively as a self-organizing community, whether peasant-indigenous movements, which have claimed the defense of land and territory for decades, or urban social movements, which are associated with the struggle for land and the demands for basic needs. However, by the year 2000, the dispute over territory met other complications, including the new methods adopted by the capitalist view of spaces considered strategic in terms of natural assets. Accordingly, extractive megaprojects, such as large-scale metal mining, the expansion of the hydro-carbon frontier, agribusiness, among others, can be thought of as a paradigmatic example in which a "tension of territorialities" is provoked (Porto Gonçalves, 2001), via the formation of a dominant vision of territoriality that is presented as excluding the existing (or potentially existing) ones. In short, various logics of territoriality could refer to the large economic actors (corporations, economic elites), the States (at their various levels) or the different social actors organized and/or involved in the conflict.

The appropriation of territory is never only material; it is also symbolic (Santos, 2005). As the Brazilian geographer Bernardo Mançano Fernandes affirmed, "we coexist with different types of territories producing and produced by distinct social relations, which are disputed daily" (2008). Undoubtedly, it has been the critical geography of Brazil that contributed to the enrichment and reformation of the concept of territory, especially given the perspective that emphasizes the need to "graph territories from within" (Porto Gonçalves, 2001), that is to say, an estimation of the territory and territoriality that social move-ments forge in their struggles. For Porto Gonçalves, our epoch can be compared to the Renaissance, in the sense that we are witnessing a process of (re) geographical configuration, where the different actors and segments of society are not present in the same way in these instituting processes.

Territoriality is carried out in a complex space, in which lines of action and rationalities bearing different assessments are intertwined. In a similar vein, another Brazilian geographer, Rogerio Haesbert (2011), reflects on multi-territoriality, which he interprets as the counterpart to globalization. Far from witnessing an "end of the territories," a more complex geography – multi-territoriality – is delineated, with strong rhizomatic connotations, that is, not hierarchized and instead illustrated by network territories established by sub-ordinate groups.

In the framework of the commodities consensus, we are witnessing a shift in the dominant notion of territory, in line with the dominant development model. Paraphrasing the geographer Robert Sack (1986), it could be said that for the sake of capital, companies and governments gauge an efficient vision of the territories, which considers them "socially desolate" as long as they contain goods valued by capital. In the name of promoting the ideology of progress, the communities settled there appear invisible, the regional economies devalued, or their crises intensified, to facilitate the entry of large projects that end up becoming agents of territorial occupation. Such processes of devaluation are exacerbated in traditionally relegated regions.

For example, in the Argentine Patagonia, vast territories are considered as "deserts," which prompts dark reminiscences, because this metaphor was used in the late nineteenth century to corral and exterminate indigenous populations, devaluing what they represented in terms of culture and habitat. Currently, government officials and provincial governments use the metaphor of the desert to prompt, for example, the need for large-scale mining or the expansion of the oil frontier through fracking or agribusiness as the only effective alternative. A similar occurrence happens with the Amazon, another relegated territory. As Porto Gonçalves (2017) affirms, it is not only considered as a "reserve of resources" or "inexhaustible source" but also as a "demographic vacuum"; the dominant classes consequently accept this concept, given their subordinate role to central world powers, ultimately ignoring the geographical complexity of the region. This efficient vision is complementary to the characterization of the territory as "idle" or "unproductive." In the Latin American context, Peruvian President Alan García, who in 2007 expressed this vision in a starker way, published the article *The Hortelano Dog Syndrome*, in the newspaper *El Comercio*, in Lima, in which he callously outlines his policy in relation to the Amazon. He argued that the Amazonian Indians who opposed the exploitation of their "idle territories" were like "the dog of the gardener." In García's words, the entire Amazon was considered an idle territory that had to become an efficient and productive area, through the expansion of the mining, energy, and oil frontiers.[17]

In short, the assertion that there are regions historically marked by poverty and social vulnerability, with a low population density, that have large areas of "unproductive" territories facilitates the establishment of an efficient and exclusive discourse on behalf of the global dynamics of capital. Whether they are conceived as "socially desolate territories," "idle," "deserts," or "empty spaces," the result is similar: the devaluation of regional economies. In other words, the use of such language regarding the valuation of the territory is linked to subordinate sectors and is increasingly incompatible with the dominant model.

The question is even more complex if we refer to the indigenous peoples and their organizations, since the ideas of territory and territoriality appear increasingly linked to the idea of autonomy, understood as self-determination, which, as affirmed by the Mexican anthropologist Héctor Díaz Polanco (2008), means not only the recognition of diversity and cultural difference but also the registration of collective, economic, and social rights within the territory.

---

[17] These statements materialized in June 2008, when the executive sanctioned a hundred legislative decrees, including the package of eleven laws affecting the Amazon. The legislative decrees, which were renamed "the law of the jungle" by indigenous organizations and environmental NGOs, would be questioned from different sectors. Finally, the repression of Bagua (June 5, 2009) cost the lives of some thirty inhabitants of the Amazon region, including police and residents.

In the context of expanding neo-extractivism, the dispute over territories had negative consequences in relation to the situation involving indigenous and peasant peoples, since a significant number of the megaprojects are situated in indigenous territories or territories claimed by indigenous peoples. A report by ECLAC on the situation of indigenous peoples, based on an investigation by the UN Special Rapporteur of the indigenous peoples (from 2009 to 2013), demonstrates one of the major nodes produced by the expansion of extractive activities in indigenous territories. According to the report, the state's (Free, Prior and Informed Consent) "failure to comply with the state's duty of consultation with indigenous peoples and for the adoption of safeguards and measures to protect their rights before granting concessions or authorizing the execution of extractive projects" (ECLAC, 2014:139). The same report identified 226 conflicts in indigenous territories of Latin America associated with extractive mining and hydrocarbon projects from 2010 to 2013 (2014: 139).

Thus, in the face of the expansion of the oil, mining, energy, and agribusiness frontiers, the territorial problems – first seen as tension, and later as antagonism – were eliciting different responses, which placed at the heart of the conflict questions regarding the right of unobstructed and informed prior consultation (henceforth FPIC). Now, with the FPIC and its implementation, there is a question that is far from being univocal, because it introduces several dilemmas: Should it be nonbinding consultation or do indigenous peoples have the right to veto? The ILO (International Labour Organization) determines that the consultation must be done in good faith and that its purpose should be to seek the consent of the community or, at least, to reach an agreement. Subsequently, in 2007, the UN Declaration on the Rights of Indigenous Peoples went a step further, involving the principle of free, prior, and informed consent for the transfer of indigenous groups from their lands, as well as for adoption and application of legislative and administrative measures that affect them. Additionally, it requires the State to restore all intellectual, cultural, or spiritual assets that the indigenous groups had lost without their free, prior, and informed consent. Finally, although these provisions are not binding, they establish a strong government commitment and exert pressure on the State to carry out this adaptation.

At that time, the Colombian specialist in indigenous rights César Rodríguez Garavito (2012:48) distinguished between strong and weak interpretations of the right of consultation. From his perspective, "international organizations such as the Rapporteurship on the Rights of Indigenous Peoples of the UN and the Inter-American Court of Human Rights have established the most demanding interpretations of international law, especially when dealing with large development or investment plans that have a profound impact on an indigenous people." At the other end of the spectrum, we have a weak procedural conception, such as the one expressed by the Constitutional Court of Ecuador (2010: 48).

An important advancement in the line of interpretation was the judgment of the IACHR (Inter-American Commission on Human Rights) of July 30, 2012, in relation to the Kichwa Sarayaku people of the Ecuadorian Amazon, where ten years before a complaint was lodged against the Ecuadorian State for having granted an oil concession and allowed a company of Argentine capitals to undertake seismic exploration in the territory of the Sarayaku people, without prior consultation.[18] The court determined that Ecuador violated the rights to prior and informed consultation, to indigenous communal property, and to cultural identity. The State was also found responsible for seriously endangering the rights to life and personal integrity, and for the violation of the rights to judicial guarantees and judicial protection to the detriment of the Sarayaku people.[19] This ruling marked a milestone in the matter and was expected to have an impact on pending litigation between indigenous rights and the expansion of the extractive frontier. Not coincidentally, since then the IACHR has been under the microscope of Latin American governments: for example, Venezuela decided to withdraw, alleging the organization's bias and moral decadence; Brazil threatened to do the same after receiving precautionary measures from the IACHR, implying the suspension of the construction of the Belo Monte mega-dam, carried out without due consultation with the indigenous populations.

With that in mind, consultations were involved in an increasingly complex and dynamic field of social and legal disputes. In the perspective of the Latin American governments, this became something more than a pebble in a shoe both for a democratizing government like that of Evo Morales,[20] who did not fail to make an openly manipulative use of the FPIC during the conflict of the TIPNIS (Isiboro Secure Indigenous Territory and National Park), and for the government of Rafael Correa in Ecuador, because despite its ratification, in

---

[18] In 2007, through five contentious cases, the IACHR established a legal international framework to settle problems between states and indigenous communities. It established that it is states' responsibility to guarantee the effective participation of indigenous communities, which must be consulted following their customary traditions. It also established that the consultations should be informed prior to the development of the projects, making sure that the communities are cognizant of the risks involved. The communities, rather than the state, must decide who will represent them in the consultation process, which must be carried out in every instance of megaprojects, when the states must obtain the prior, free, and informed consent of the affected communities.

[19] www.escr-net.org/es/caselaw/2012/caso-pueblo-indigena-kichwa-sarayaku-vs-ecuador

[20] In Bolivia, the FPIC started in 2007. "Between 2007 and 2017, the Ministry of Hydrocarbons and Energy . . . led fifty-eight consultations prior to the extraction of gas in territories of indigenous original nations and peasant communities. The available information on these processes is incomplete, but government documents, news media, case studies, and interviews indicate they involved contracts with a handful of large corporations, including the nationalized YPFB and its subsidiaries" (Falleti and Riofrancos, 2018: 104).

practice it was not fulfilled, interpreted simply as "pre-legislative consultation." In Peru, the various neoliberal governments sought to place a brake (often violent) on the demand for the right of consultation, trying to limit it to the Amazonian peoples, to the detriment of the Andean communities, where the mining projects resided. Also, in Argentina, strategic laws on natural resources were approved (such as the non-conventional hydrocarbons law, in 2014) without incorporating consultation with indigenous peoples, who are considered not owners, but "superficial" (Svampa, 2018a). Overall, there was no Latin American government that did not attempt to minimize the FPIC, to limit it to its weakest version, through different legislations and regulations, whose purpose was to establish its nonbinding character, as well as to facilitate protection or manipulation, in contexts of strong asymmetry of powers.

At the regional level, in terms of territorial tension, the TIPNIS conflict was one of the most resounding. Although several episodes anticipated a collision between the indigenous narrative and the neo-extractivist practice of the government of Evo Morales, the turning point occurred between 2010 and 2011, following the construction of the Villa Tunari–San Ignacio highway. TIPNIS has been a natural reserve since 1965; since 1990, it has been recognized as an indigenous territory, a habitat for Amazonian peoples. The question is undoubtedly complex: on the one hand, the project responded to geopolitical and territorial needs; yet on the other hand, the indigenous peoples involved were not consulted. Likewise, the highway would open the door to extractive projects, with the negative social, cultural, and environmental consequences, with or without Brazil as a strategic ally. In short, the escalation of the conflict between indigenous and environmental organizations and the government was such that it included several marches from the TIPNIS to the city of La Paz; the articulation of a multi-sectoral block of rural, social, and environmental indigenous organizations, with the support of huge urban sectors; in addition to a dark repressive episode led by State forces (In September 2011 Bolivian police raided an encampment of several hundred indigenous people gathered to protest the government's plan to build a road through their lands). In 2012, the government of Evo Morales called for a study of the TIPNIS communities; the official report indicated that 80 percent of the communities consulted approved the construction of the highway. However, a report by the Catholic Church, carried out with the Permanent Assembly of Human Rights of Bolivia in April 2013, indicated that the consultation with the indigenous people "was not free or in good faith, besides it did not conform to the standards of prior consultation and it was done with perks."[21]

---

[21] http://cidob-bo.org/index.php?option=com_content&view=article&id=2014:obispos-defienden-su-informe-de-la-consulta-previa-en-el-tipnis&catid=82:noticias&Itemid=2

The TIPNIS conflict settled two important issues that should be interpreted as a Bolivian, but also Latin American, key: first, this conflict whitewashed the Bolivian government's discourse on its definition of development, something explicitly stated by Vice President Alvaro García Linera in his book *Geopolítica de la Amazonia* (2012). Second, in a context of escalation of the conflict, in such virulent and politicized contexts – where the recursive character of the action leads to the different actors getting involved in a fierce struggle – the possibility of carrying out a free, prior, and informed consultation with indigenous peoples – according to ILO Convention 169 – is inevitably endangered, and the definition of its procedures, mechanisms, and issues ends up being controversial.[22]

Overall, the issue of the FPIC turned out to be one of the most difficult and controversial problems of international, regional, and national regulations related to the rights of indigenous peoples. Although it appears as "a specialized instrument," (because it requires legal knowledge), in just two decades it has been subject to legal conflicts in which large economic interests as well as the survival of indigenous peoples and other ethnic groups are challenged. At the same time, it is clear that the expansion of the frontier of collective and territorial rights of native peoples found a clear limit in the growing expansion of the borders of exploitation of capital, in search of goods, lands, and territories, which threw into the air the emancipatory narratives that had raised strong expectations, especially in countries like Bolivia and Ecuador.

2.3 Socio-environmental Conflicts, Eco-territorial Turn, and Social Organizations

It could be perceived that the consolidation of an alternative valuation language to that of the dominant territoriality is more immediate in the case of indigenous and peasant organizations, as a result of the close relationship they pose between land and territory and in community life terms, such as the well-known reactivation of the indigenous community matrix that occurred in recent decades. However, rather than omit the countries in which there is a presence of indigenous peoples who have been historically excluded, the new language of valuation of the territory also covers other countries in which it is expressed through different multiethnic experiences and various organizational formats.

These new socio-environmental, rural, and urban movements (in small and medium-sized localities) of a poly-classist nature are characterized by an

---

[22] Another limitation of the FPIC is that successive decrees limit the time that the consultation can last. In Bolivia, following the hydrocarbons law and other decrees that provided the regulatory framework, prior consultation in hydrocarbons and mining cannot last more than three months in total (Falleti and Riofrancos, 2018).

assembly format and a potentially important antagonistic potential. It should be noted that in this new social fabric, different cultural groups, certain environmental NGOs (with logic of social movements), intellectuals, and experts, who accompany – and can even be co-protagonists – the action of social organizations and movement plays an important role. As often happens in other areas of conflict, the organizational dynamics have young central actors, many of them women, whose role is crucial both in the large organizational structures and in the small groups. The crossings and articulations between organizations gave rise to numerous coordination spaces, thematic forums – in defense of water, of rivers, and of natural assets – and joint action platforms (against the FTAA, against fracking, against megaprojects of the IIRSA, and against the TransPacific Treaty).

It is difficult to carry out an exhaustive survey of the self-organizational, national, and regional networks of socio-environmentalists that characterize Latin America. By way of example, I present a brief review of some socio-environmental conflicts and networks in countries such as Peru, Bolivia, Ecuador, Colombia, Mexico, Nicaragua, Venezuela, and Argentina. In 2013, in Peru, a country with a tradition of large-scale mining, according to the Ombudsman's Office (An Ombudsman or public advocate is an official who is charged with representing the interests of the public by investigating and addressing complaints of maladministration or a violation of rights. In Peru is the Ombudsman who publish the social conflicts in the country). Out of a total of 120 conflicts, those linked to mining represented 48 percent of all social conflicts.[23] In 2016, the percentage had risen to 68 percent, since there were already 220 social conflicts that the Peruvian authorities had identified throughout the national territory, of which 150 were related to the imposition of mining projects. Among the pioneering organizations at the continental level in the fight against mega-mining, the National Confederation of Communities Affected by Mining (CONACAMI), established in 1999, stands out. It maintained a territorial presence and articulation capacity until 2008–2009. Currently, other local organizational structures have been strengthened, such as the peasant patrols (Hoetmer et al., 2013: 268).

In Bolivia, the extractive wave includes mining, hydrocarbon exploitation, the advancement of agribusiness, and more recently a series of energy projects included in the so-called 2025 Patriotic Agenda, a new National Development Plan, that involves the construction of several mega-dams and a nuclear power plant in El Alto. As has been previously mentioned, the watershed was the conflict of the TIPNIS, from which many others followed. In 2015, Vice

---

[23] www.defensoria.gob.pe/blog/mineria-y-conflictos/

President Garcia Linera threatened to expel four Bolivian NGOs (CEDIB, Terra, CEDLA, and Milenio), recognized leftist organizations conducting research on neo-extractivism and the expansion of the agribusiness frontier. Linera accused them of defending "the interests of the international political right." In 2016, the government enacted a new law that aimed to restrict freedom of association and put critical NGOs at risk of closure if they did not comply with the 2025 Patriotic Agenda and the National Development Plan. In 2017, the harassment and persecution of one of them, the CEDIB, renowned national documentation center, was so persistent that its operation became almost unsustainable.

One of the most worrisome cases is Ecuador. Although its constitution establishes the rights of nature, the response of the Correa government to the conflict was the criminalization and judicialization of environmental protest. Criminal trials sentenced spokespeople for indigenous organizations to up to ten years imprisonment,[24] as well as the withdrawal of legal status and the expulsion of NGOs (Fundación Pachamama, 2013), harassment and threat of dissolution of the recognized NGO Acción Ecológica in 2009 and 2016, and the cancellation of visas and expulsion of foreign consultants linked to environmental leaders in 2014 and 2015. Also, the Ecuadorian government used legal devices to invalidate the demand for popular initiative, which provoked the citizen movement "Yasunidos," after the government decided unilaterally to end the moratorium in the Yasuni Park and begin oil exploitation. Despite the significant resistance against mega-mining (Ecuador has no tradition of large-scale mining), from 2013 the government continued the with the intervention of the Ecuadorian police forces, including Intag, a stronghold in the fight against this type of activity, where the population expelled several mining companies, betting on alternative development. Alongside this, it should be noted that Chinese companies, which lead the mining investment in Ecuador, have been accused of abusive labor practices. According to Ong Acción Ecológica, in 2012 the Shuar community denounced Chinese companies linked to the Mirador mining project for breaches of labor benefits, employee mistreatment, unfair wages, and work-related accidents. In 2016, new conflicts arose when Shuar indigenous people seized a mining camp in the Amazon region, arguing that the entry of the Chinese company was carried out without prior consultation and militarization of the territories. The level of the conflict escalated and resulted in one death and several people wounded. President Correa then

---

[24] See the report of the FIDH, which includes cases of criminalization of human rights defenders in Latin America, among them cases of criminalization in Intag and the indigenous people of the Shuar Federation (2015). www.fidh.org/IMG/pdf/criminalisationobsangocto2015bassdef.pdf

declared a state of emergency and accused the Shuar Indians of being a "paramilitary and semi-criminal group."

Likewise, in Colombia, between 2001 and 2011, 25 percent of socio-environmental conflicts were related to oil, gold, and coal (Roa Avendaño and Navas, 2014: 35). In 2010, during his first presidential campaign, José Manuel Santos launched the slogan "Colombia the mining-energy locomotive." In that country, one of the mining projects that provoked greater resistance is La Colosa, ran by the company Anglo Gold Ashanti. If the mine had been built, it would have been the fifth-largest gold mine in the world, affecting several localities in the Tolima Department, which is considered the agricultural pantry of Colombia. There, Environmental Committees in Defense of Life were created, which promoted public consultations. After a preliminary consultation in the small town of Piedras, in 2013, the environmental committees set out to organize consultations in Cajamarca and Ibagué, finding serious legal and business obstacles. Finally, in April 2017, a public consultation was held in Cajamarca, which also yielded a negative response for La Colosa. In the absence of a social license, Anglo Gold Ashanti decided to suspend all project activities.

But mega-mining is not the only extractivist conflict in Colombia. There is also the Master Plan for the Development of the Magdalena River, the most important river in the country, which is born in the mountain range and has a length of 1500 km (932 m). The concession of the river is part of the policy from the Integration of Regional Infrastructure South American (IIRSA/COSIPLAN); rather than improve the environmental and social conditions of the river, it aims to turn it into a large waterway to transport coal, oil, and palm leaf with deep draft vessels for exportation. Another objective is to turn it into a great generator of energy, through the construction of several dams, many of which would be at the service of the mining projects. This enormous plan of privatization of the Magdalena River (controlled by a company based in China) has led to a social mobilization that goes by the name "The River of Life."

In Mexico, the National Assembly of Environmentally Affected People (ANAA, Mexico) was created in 2008 to fight against mega-mining, hydro-electric dams, urbanization, and industrial mega-dams. It is composed of pioneering coalitions such as the Council of Ejidos and Communities (CECOP), which is opposed to the La Perota Dam and for ten years united the struggling indigenous peasants in Guerrero under the slogan "We are the custodians of water" (Navarro, 2015: 141). Another important coalition is the Frente Amplio Opositor (FAO), which protests the mining company San Xavier and serves as a platform for numerous public activities, information rounds, consultations, and legal disputes. The FAO's main objective, which culminated in 2006, was to protest San Xavier's plan to build the bases of a deposit that was initially planned to demolish the town (Composto and Navarro, 2011: 51).

On the other hand, Nicaragua has one of the most ambitious yet controversial megaprojects in the region, the Interoceanic Canal, three times larger than the Panama Canal, contracted to the Chinese company HKND. In November 2015, peasant protests and the probing of the environmental impact study by international experts convened by the Nicaraguan Academy of Sciences delayead the start of the project. As a result, the National Council for the Defense of Land, Lake, and National Sovereignty was born. The first protest by the affected communities occurred in 2014. At the end of 2016, the police and the military repressed a peasant march against the canal project that was intended to reach Managua; the encounter resulted in numerous bullet wounds and detainees. However, the protest prevented the commencement of a project that would have affected numerous communities and would have serious impacts on Lake Nicaragua, the largest freshwater reserve in the region.

After the fall of commodity prices, Venezuela, a rentier country that depends on oil exports, also made a new extractivist turn. As E. Lander (2013) points out, the main trigger – although not the only one – of the crisis in that country was the drastic fall in the international price of oil. Despite having an eminently oil-based economy, mining was the activity that generated the most socio-environmental conflicts. According to the database of the Observatory of Political Ecology of Venezuela, mining initiatives generate 37 percent of the total of registered cases. Alongside mining being responsible for the most intense conflicts in the country, gold was the most disputed commodity. Likewise, the Maduro government initiated an intensive search for foreign exchange and in line with the Plan de la Patria (2013–2019), and in February 2016, it created by decree a New National Strategic Development Zone: Arco Minero del Orinoco, which opened almost 112,000 km^2 (43.2 m^2), 12 percent of the national territory, to the large mining industry for the exploitation of gold, diamonds, coltan, iron, and other minerals. To attract foreign investments, the government signed alliances and agreements with 150 national and transnational companies. The content of these agreements is unknown – decreeing a state of emergency allows the contracts for the Mining Arc to have discretion and do not require obtaining authorization from the National Assembly. In this context, mega-mining was presented as a new "miracle" exit in the search for the diversification of oil extractivism during the crisis. According to Terán Mantovani (2016:261), this would redesign the neo-extractivism cartography, in which "the new border appropriation exceeds the historical map and expands into areas of natural reserves, *offshore* extractions and national parks."

Finally, in Argentina the assemblies in defense of the water supply stand out, most of them nucleated in the Union of Citizen Assemblies (UAC, emerging in 2006) originally linked to the fight against mega-mining but also including criticism of the agribusiness model. This has an assembly format and meets three times a year, with the aim of designing common strategies of resistance against the advance of the mining model in twelve provinces and defending provincial laws (seven, in total) that prohibit mega-mining in that country. Regarding agribusiness, linked to the expansion of transgenic soybeans, the heart of agrarian capitalism in Argentina, resistances have been more difficult to conceptualize, despite the pioneering role of the Madres del Barrio Ituzaingó, in the province of Córdoba. In this process of awareness, the role of physicians and researchers, such as Andrés Carrasco, and other professionals who created the University Network of Physicians of Fumigated People, was crucial (Svampa and Viale, 2014).

2.4 The Escalation of Extractive Violence

As has been mentioned previously, in 2008–2010, we witnessed an upsurge of extractive projects, something that is reflected in the various national development plans that were part of the electoral platforms of some Latin American leaders. The counterpart to this process has been the increase in conflict, which contributed to the criminalization of socio-environmental struggles and the increase in State and parastatal violence. In this regard, we must remember that Latin America has another unfortunate ranking, because it is the region of the world where more human rights defenders and environmental activists have been assassinated, sinister indicators that have worsened in the past ten years and match the expansion of the extractive frontier and the criminalization of socio-environmental protests.

According to Global Witness (2014), between 2002 and 2013 there were 908 documented killings of environmental activists around the world, of which 83.7 percent (760 cases) have taken place in Latin America. The data also show that the increase occurred from 2007 and even more from 2009, which coincides with the multiplication stage of the extractive projects, as reflected in the development programs presented by various Latin American governments. After Brazil (50 deaths) and the Philippines (33), the third in the ranking is Colombia, with 26 killings of environmental defenders in 2015. The regional list includes countries such as Honduras, Nicaragua, Panama, Mexico, Guatemala, and Peru. At the beginning of 2012, strong movements of repression in Panama cost the lives of two members of the indigenous Ngäbe Buglé community. In Peru, during the government of Ollanta Humala (2011–2016), repression led to 25 deaths, mainly in the Cajamarca region, where villagers mobilized against the Conga Project. In 2016 and 2017, a total of 200 environmental activists were murdered, of which 60 percent were registered in Latin America. Also, in Argentina, under the neoliberal government of Mauricio Macri, during 2017, State forces killed activist Rafael Nahuel, of Mapuche origin, and another young man, Santiago Maldonado, died by drowning as a result of state repression.

Additionally, the increase in State and parastatal violence against women who oppose neo-extractivism must be recognized. Most of the attacks were carried out in contexts of forced eviction; police forces or paramilitary groups physically and sexually violated women (FAU-AL 2016). In March 2016, the well-known leader Berta Cáceres was assassinated in Honduras by repressive government forces for opposing a hydroelectric dam. In January 2017, feminist and activist against mega-mining Laura Vasquez Pineda, member of the Ancestral Community Healing Network of Guatemala, was murdered.

No less serious is the combination of political patronage and extractivist violence that marks the strong relationship between the Bolivian government and the powerful mining cooperatives in disputes over surplus, once the period of extraordinary profitability ended. The murder in 2016 of Deputy Minister Rodolfo Illanes, at the hands of mining cooperative members, in retaliation for police repression, was news that had a great national and international impact. It was undoubtedly an extractive war, because what was at stake, in a context of falling international mineral prices, was the control of the surplus. Although having instigated the process but unable to control it, the government of Evo Morales had to face a model of excessive corporatism, which he had reinforced through economic privileges in exchange for political support.[25]

Thus, the opening of a new cycle of violation of human rights highlights the limitation of the models of democratic governance now implemented in the region as well as the retraction of the borders of rights. This includes both the violation of basic political rights – the right to information, the right to demonstrate, the right to participate in collective decisions (consultations, referendums) – as well as the violation of territorial and environmental rights

---

[25] Many of these associations are not even cooperatives, but covert private companies that outsource labor, in conditions of over-exploitation, which include extensive working hours (up to sixteen hours a day), while selling the extracted material to transnational companies. According to the CEDIB, there are between 100,000 and 120,000 cooperative miners, but an important sector (between 40 percent and 50 percent) is subcontracted. Thus, the reality shows the emergence of a proprietary sector enriched thanks to the conditions of exploitation and the high prices of minerals during the super cycle of commodities. After gas, mining today represents the second source of wealth in Bolivia with 25 percent of exports, which include tin, zinc, silver, copper, and gold. The economic boom enabled the cooperatives to increase, going from 500 in 2005 to 1600 in 2015.

(over indigenous and non-indigenous individuals), present in the new constitutions and in national and international legislation

In short, neo-extractivism is increasingly taking victims, particularly in Latin America, a region that holds the world record for murders of environmental activists. As in other times, the *eldoradista* narrative is turning into a renewed dialect of plunder and dependence, which is accompanied by increased extractivism, increased violence, and therefore less democracy. Nothing indicates that these indexes will improve – rather, quite the opposite, if we take into account the current conservative turn, illustrated by countries such as Argentina and Brazil, whose current governments not only deepened the extractivist model in all its versions, accentuating state violence on the most vulnerable populations, but also enacted a series of public policies that entail a significant regression in terms of social rights.

3 Topics and Debates Regarding the Eco-territorial Turn

3.1 From the Eco-territorial Turn and the Limits to the Questioning of Neo-extractivism

Beyond the specific markings, the dynamics of socio-environmental struggles in Latin America have laid the foundations of a common language of valuation on territoriality, which increasingly accounts for the innovative intersection between the indigenous-community matrix and environmental discourse. This convergence expresses what we can call an eco-territorial turn, which is a realization of the way in which one thinks and demonstrates from the perspective of the collective resistances and the current socio-environmental struggles centered on the defense of land and territory.

A preliminary matter to take into account is that the eco-territorial turn refers to the construction of collective action frameworks, which function both as structures of meaning and schemes of alternative interpretation as collective subjectivity producers. These collective frameworks tend to develop an important mobilizing capacity; they install new themes, languages, and slogans, in terms of societal debates, while orienting the interactive dynamic toward the construction of a common subjectivity in the Latin American space of struggles.

In this context, the most novel aspect is the articulation by different actors (indigenous-peasant movements, socio-environmental movements, environmentalist NGOs, networks of intellectuals and experts, cultural collectives), which translates into a dialogue of knowledge and disciplines, leading to the emergence of an expert knowledge independent of the dominant discourses, and to the valorization of local knowledge, much of it with peasant-indigenous roots. The issue is not minor, because from this acknowledgment, different organizations and movements elaborate common diagnoses, expand the discursive platform (which exceeds local and national problems), and diversify the strategies to combat the issue. This enables linkage of grassroots mobilization with social networks to create and apply novel technical and legal instruments (to promote collective protection, new ordinances, demand for public consultation, and laws for the protection of the environment and the rights of indigenous peoples).

The fight has allowed for the establishment of other languages of valuation of the territory, other ways of building the link with nature, and other narratives of the earth that recreate a relational paradigm based on reciprocity, complementarity, and care. These point to various modes of appropriation, a widened dialogue of knowledge, and other forms of social organizations. Such languages stem from different political-ideological matrices – anti-capitalist, ecologist and indigenous, feminist, and anti-patriarchal perspectives – that originate from the heterogeneous world of the subaltern classes.

The eco-territorial turn also presents significant connections with the environmental justice movements that originated in the 1980s in African American communities in the United States. Such an approach "implies the right to a safe, healthy and productive environment for all, where the environment is considered in its entirety, including its ecological, physical, constructed, social, political, aesthetic and economic dimensions" (Acselard, 2004: 16). This is a common philosophy at the inception of various environmental justice networks that are currently being developed in Latin America, in countries such as Chile (OLCA) and Brazil (Environmental Justice Network).[26]

From my perspective, the wide-ranging topics of the eco-territorial turn account for the emergence of a new system of struggles, with the gestation of an alternative language that has strong resonance within the Latin American space of struggles. This common framework of meaning articulates indigenous struggles, territorial-ecological militancy, and feminist perspectives, which reveal an expansion of the socially established boundaries, in opposition to the dominant model. Given that it is a rhetoric of defense of the territory and the common goods, of human rights, of the rights of nature, or of *Buen Vivir*, the demand points to a democratization of decision making when faced with projects that seriously affect the conditions of life of the most vulnerable sectors and compromise future generations.

However, it would be a mistake to interpret these collective frameworks as if they were univocal or encompassed all experiences, given the heterogeneity of

---

[26] The following sites can be consulted: www.olca.cl/oca/justicia/justicia02.htm and www.justicaambiental.org.br/_justicaambiental

organizations and traditions of struggle. More simply put, it is necessary to read the eco-territorial turn as a trend that runs through the struggles and constructs a more generally intelligible framework. For this reason, emblematic socio-environmental conflicts (especially during the second phase of neo-extractivism described earlier) contributed to raising awareness, expanding the debate to include environmental issues, even if most governments and a multitude of social sectors in urban areas tend to understand it in a narrow or partial manner. By such parties viewing it as just another dimension, they fail to recognize the multiple implications that neo-extractivism brings.[27]

In other words, although the latest trend is the rejection of neo-extractive projects and the development of other valuation languages, it is also true that many populations accept economic compensation or await the "economic spill" promised by the government and corporations. For example, although extractivism and particularly mining have a long and dark history in Latin America, in those countries where there is a strong mining tradition, as in Bolivia and Peru, the tendency has been to adopt an imagined concession to associate mining and development. Referring to Peru, the English geographer Anthony Bebbington (2009) argues that there would be a dividing line between those who end up betting on some form of compensation, as a way to resolve the conflict, and others who reject mining, question the development model, and tend to rethink the rules of the game. However, it is also possible to find, in an ambiguous way, both positions in social movements. For others, like the Peruvian Vladimir Pinto Palacio Paéz and Hoetmer (2008), in reality, there would be two central positions. In old mining areas, despite the strong criticism of the companies, the demands of the population were directed to reform the previous working and environmental conditions since the economic, social, and cultural rights affected by the presence of mining were recognized. The other is the position in regions where there was no history of mining activity, which explains why these populations would show greater resistance (Tambogrande, Huancabamba, Ayavaca, among others). The truth is that with respect to open-pit mining, where there is no large-scale mining tradition, with their *eldoradista* narrative associated with progress and development, in general, populations tend to reject the activity and assume more radical positions.

Additionally, it is necessary to recognize that the process of territorial construction takes place in a complex space, in which lines of action and rationalities carrying different valuations are intertwined. We have already spoken

---

[27] The constitution of some socio-environmental conflicts as "emblematic cases" is important for collective action, not only because of their public visibility but also because of the degree of contestation they convey, for what they express in terms of a new line of accumulation of struggles associated with a counterhegemonic narrative.

about the tension of territorialities. Bear in mind that an important part of the organizations involved in the socio-environmental struggles reside in rural territories, perhaps semi-isolated, where peasant and indigenous populations live, whose power of pressure is weak compared to that of the large urban centers. In any case, the distance from the big cities helped reinforce disconnections between the countryside and city; the mountains, the jungle, and the coast, as in Peru and Colombia; or between small towns and large cities in Argentina, where the extent to which megaprojects (mining, oil, agribusiness, dams) seems to indirectly affect large cities. Consequently, there is a disconnect between the organizations and movements that denounce the extractivist logic and the trade unions and socio-territorial organizations that are located in the large urban centers and have a representative presence on the national political scene.

3.2 Relational Matrices: The Debates on Good Living and Environmental Rights

One of the most collective themes that has been subject to Latin American critical thinking and has given greater vitality to the current eco-territorial turn is the *Buen Vivir* (BV), *sumak kawsay* and *suma qamaña* in Quechua and Aymara, respectively. Although linked to the Andean indigenous cosmovision, the concept of BV quickly took on continental and global resonances

BV has as one of its central axes the relationship between human beings and nature. It includes other valuation rhetoric (ecological, religious, aesthetic, cultural) related to nature that claims economic growth must be subject to the conservation of life. This perspective results, therefore, in the recognition of the rights of nature (Gudynas, 2015), which does not imply untouched nature but integral respect for its existence; the defense of ecosystems; and the maintenance and regeneration of its life cycles, structure, functions, and evolutionary processes. The rights of nature introduce a profound societal change, which questions the dominant anthropocentric logic and becomes a vanguard response to the current civilizational crisis. Thus, in line with the principles of the BV, emphasis should be placed on building a society based on harmonious relationships between human beings and nature. Thus, if development aims to "Westernize" life on the planet, BV salvages the values of diversity and respect for one another (Acosta, 2013).

In its different versions, BV is a recent social-historical construction,[28] although it maintains its long-term meaning, which includes the sense of

---

[28] The Ecuadorean anthropologist David Cortes (2012), who has been tracing the genealogy of BV, maintains that there is no explicit record of this term prior to 2000, nor references in any chronicle or dictionary of Quechua or Aymara language.

maintaining indigenous communities in their relational and communal world-view, which is opposed to modern Western logic. The explicit references to BV appear around 2000 in Bolivia, from indigenous intellectuals like Simon Yampara (2004) and toward 2001, in Ecuador, with the economist Alberto Acosta and the indigenous leader Carlos Viteri from the Kichua peoples of Sarayaku. The issue finds a major impulse in the framework of the constituent debates in Bolivia and Ecuador. In this context, BV appears as a broad area in which different emancipatory meanings are inscribed, where the indigenous community comprised both the inspiring framework and the common core. In Ecuador, BV is read as a plural concept, endowing itself with a long lineage (ranging from Aristotle to eco-socialism and ecofeminism); however, in Bolivia, it has a more restricted use linked to the vision of the original peoples.

From the philosophical point of view, the concept of BV proposes a holistic relational vision, whether it connects with a paradigm of the indigenous world-view or whether it reaches its maximum power linked to other visions of nature. Rights of nature are included in the new constitution of Ecuador and defined as "the right to be fully respected [in] its existence, and the maintenance and regeneration of its life cycles, structure, functions and evolutionary processes" (Article 71).

The association between BV and rights of nature has several consequences. First, the new paradigm points to a progressive process of de-commodification of nature. Second, it recognizes intrinsic or proper values of nature independent of human valuation (Gudynas, 2013, Svampa and Viale, 2014). Third, nature as a subject of law requires a relationship of equality between humanity and nature, which forces nature to be recognized as a life to be respected. Fourth, it urges the creation of another field of justice, ecological justice, whose objective is not to collect fines for the damage caused but is environmental (re)compensation regardless of its economic cost. The criterion of justice will focus on ensuring vital processes and not on economic benefit (Gudynas, 2013: 273–74). Consequently, the aim is to expand and complete the human rights paradigm (anthropocentric vision), including the rights of nature (biocentric vision). For Alberto Acosta (2011), this movement aims to preserve the integrity of natural processes, guaranteeing the flow of energy and materials in the biosphere, while preserving the planet's biodiversity.

Although BV is a "concept under construction" in a disputed space, from the beginning there was the risk of its vampirization or distortion. Until 2010, BV demands entailed a radical criticism of the modern development program and, therefore, implied a questioning of Western modernity, in defense of the *Pachamama* or the rights of nature. There was thus a consensus that BV posed alternative measures to the conventional path of development, which opened a possibility to think about the transition and exit of neo-extractivism. However, in the heat of the progressive political cycle, a shift was occurring based on the idea of civilizational change and BV toward socialism, in a modern Western key (Lander, 2013: 18).

In short, from my perspective two breaks can be detected. On the one hand, from the progressive governments, BV was distorted, dissociating itself from the idea of the rights of nature or the *Pachamama*, to be relinked to more conventional optics, for example, to human development (the "capability approach"), as happened in Ecuador. On the other hand, due to the outbreak of contradictions, both in Bolivia and Ecuador, some authors identified in the indigenous perspective sought to establish a difference – the "bifurcation" – between BV or "living well," which they associate not only with the governmental positions but also with critical intellectual perspectives (which they consider essentially as "eclectic") and *sumak kawsay* and *suma qamaña*, in an Amerindian key, which they link with indigenous and peasant organizations and subjects.[29] The reality is that the political debates about BV created such a rupture that at the end of the progressive cycle, it was dissociated from the rights of nature and turned into a battlefield between different meanings and appropriations. Consequently, the concept of BV lost part of its aura and its disruptive capacity.

On another front, there is a close connection between the rights of nature and the valuation of relational approaches. The importance of this topic is not minor, since it assumes a different perspective to the Western dualist paradigm, which establishes a hiatus between society and nature, human and nonhuman. As Arturo Escobar (2011) argues, the problem is not that there are dualistic visions, but rather the cultural forms in which the binary pair is treated, that is, the hierarchies or asymmetries that are established (man/woman, nature/culture, civilized/barbarian, modern/traditional). This hierarchical classification of differences is one of the features of what in Latin America is called "coloniality of power" (Quijano, 2014), which leads to the suppression and elimination of other forms of knowledge and culture. In the same token, in the middle of the socioecological crisis, the critical anthropology of the past decades reminds us of the existence of other forms of construction of the link with nature, between the human and the nonhuman. In other words: not all cultures or all historical times, even in the West, developed a dualistic approach to nature, considering it a separate, external environment, at the service of human beings and their predatory eagerness. The societal crisis forces us to abdicate from the single thought, to assume diversity in terms not only epistemological but also

---

[29] Svampa, 2016: 396–397

ontological. There are other matrices of a generative type, based on a more dynamic and relational vision, as is the case in some Eastern cultures, where the concepts of movement and of becoming are the principles that govern the world and are embodied in nature, or those immanentistic visions of the indigenous peoples who perceived humankind as immersed in nature rather than separated from it.

These relational approaches, which emphasize the interdependence of the living, account for other forms of relationships between living beings, take different names: animism, for Philippe Descola (2005) or *perspectivismo amerindio* (Amerindian perspectivism), for Eduardo Viveiros de Castro (2013), who in his essay *La Mirada del Jaguar* conceptualizes the local Amazonian model of relationship with nature:

> It is about the notion, first of all, that the world is populated by many species of beings (besides the humans themselves) endowed with conscience and culture and, secondly, that each of these species sees itself and the other species in a rather unique way: each one sees herself as human, seeing others as non-human, that is, as species of animals or spirits. (Viveiros de Castro, 2013: 16)

In contrast to the modern vision, the common ground between humans and nonhumans "is not animality, but humanity" (Viveiros de Castro, 2008: 56–57). Therefore, humanity does not become the exception, but the rule; each species sees itself as human, therefore, as subject, under the species of culture. These forms of relationship and appropriation of nature question the constitutive dualisms of modernity. These "relational ontologies," as Arturo Escobar (2014) calls them after the anthropologist Mario Blaser, have the territory and its communal logics as a condition of possibility. In different latitudes, they gave rise to a profuse anthropological literature on the "ontological turn."[30]

Finally, the opening to a relational approach also connects to the Anthropocene concept. Certainly, various scholars agree that entering an era marked by the increasing consumption of fossil fuels has generated a major change, the Era of the Anthropocene, a concept coined by P. Crutzen, in 2000, to account for the existence of a new "geological epoch dominated on different scales by man" (Bonneuil and Fressoz, 2013:38). The Anthropocene concept became a point of convergence among geologists, ecologists, climate and earth system specialists, historians, philosophers, citizens, and environmentalists to jointly think about this age in which humanity has become a major geological force due to several factors, including climate change, produced by the degree of concentration of CO_2 in the atmosphere, which in turn results

---

[30] Véase Tola, 2016 and Holbraad and Pedersen, 2017.

from the burning of fossil fuels and deforestation. We would then find our-selves facing the problem of civilizing limits, within the framework of a finite and humanly modified planet, which demands the need to think from other bases on the relationship between society and nature; between economy and politics; between production, circulation, and consumption of goods. In its most critical versions, the anthropogenic turn questions the cultural paradigm of modernity, based on an instrumental vision of nature, functional to the logic of expansion of capital.

3.3 The Defense of Common Goods and Female Protagonists

Another topic of the eco-territorial turn refers to conceiving natural goods as "commons" (*bienes communes* in Spanish), one of the keys in the search for an alternative paradigm both in the North and in the Global South. The discussion of the concept of "commons" has been unfolding in two registers. At the first level, there is the question of de-commodification. This refers to the need to keep out of the market those resources and goods that, because of their natural, social, and cultural heritage, belong to the community and have a value that exceeds any price. But the notion of common goods does not only imply a rejection of the logic of commodities but also aims to place in debate the statist vision of "natural resources," based on the construction of a type of territoriality based on the protection of the natural, social, and cultural heritage of "the common."

The second dimension, which refers to the paradigm of common goods, is based on the production and reproduction of the commons. This poses a different perspective on social relations, from the configuration or emergence of spaces and forms of social cooperation, of common use and enjoyment, in the sense of what Mexican Gustavo Esteva (2007) characterized as "areas of community." Belgian François Houtart (2011) associates the commons with the common good of humanity, due to its general nature, which implies the foundations of the collective life of humanity on the planet: the relationship with nature; the production of life; collective organization (politics); and the reading, evaluation, and expression of reality (culture). In short, the common good of humanity is life and its reproduction.

At the second level, when reconfiguring the link with nature from a relational perspective, undoubtedly the ethics of care and ecofeminism open up alterna-tives. Historically, the role of women in social struggles in the Global South has been important. Authors such as Hindu essayist and feminist Vandana Shiva (2005) refer to the growing importance of southern feminism, so there would be an "ecofeminism of survival" (known in Spanish as *Ecofeminismo de la supervivencia)* linked to the diverse experiences of women in the defense of health, survival, and territory, which led to the awareness of solid links between women and environmentalism, feminism and ecology.

In Latin America, the presence of female protagonists had increased in the past decades: indigenous women, rural women, poor rural and urban women, women of African-diaspora descent, lesbians and trans women have all found their voices and mobilized and are dedicated to reinforcing relationships of solidarity and new forms of collective self-management. To account for this empowerment, *popular feminists* are increasingly associated with the most marginalized sectors and tend to question the individualist and modern Western view in favor of greater appreciation of "collective and community experience" (Korol, 2016). Among the popular feminist symbols in the region are *community feminists* (known in Spanish as *feminismos comunitarios)* who emphasize the existence of other forms of modernity, different from the dominant Western one, linking decolonization with de-patriarchization. Inside this community is great diversity, from feminist groups that link patriarchy with colonial history and others that, far from an idealization of the community, highlight its "(re)functionalization" (Lorena Cabnal, Guatemalan Xinka feminist) or its "colonial junction" (Julieta Paredes, Feminist Assembly, Bolivia), within the framework of the current peasant-indigenous communities (Gargallo Celentani, 2015; Svampa, 2017).

Currently, popular feminists are reflected in socio-environmental struggles in their different modalities. By way of example, we can highlight Argentina, where the movement of "Las madres del Barrio Ituzaingó," from the city of Córdoba, was a pioneer in denouncing the impact of the herbicide glyphosate on health, which led to the first criminal trial on this subject (Svampa and Viale, 2014). It is worth noting the persistence of the women of the Assembly of Chilecito and Famatina (teachers, housewives, merchants), who resisted the onslaught of the mining corporations (expelling four companies, between 2009 and 2015), as well as the resistance of Mapuche women against fracking in Neuquén. From Chile comes the example of the "Women of Zones of Sacrifice in Resistance of Quintero-Puchuncaví," (this refers a group of women who report a situation of environmental injustice, in highly polluted areas.) in an industrial pole near Valparaíso, a phenomenon analyzed by Paola Bolados and Alejandra Sanchez Cuevas (2017) in terms of "feminist political ecology" and "environmental violence." The same can be said of Colombia about the resistance of women to the expansion of the oil frontier (Roa Avendaño and Scandizzo, 2017). These are just some examples, but the fact is that women's protagonist role in the eco-territorial struggles is a repeated occurrence in all the countries of the region.

The contributions of popular feminists, in an ecological key, contribute to questioning the reductionist vision based on the idea of autonomy and individualism. Certainly, the ethics of care places independence as the central focus, which in the key of civilizational crisis is read as eco-dependence. The revaluation and universalization of the ethics of care, seen as a relational faculty that patriarchy has essentialized (in relation to women) or disconnected (in relation to men), as Carol Gilligan (2015) states, opens up a process of liberation greater not only of feminism but also of all humanity. The processual dynamics of the struggles also involve a questioning of patriarchy, based on a binary and hierarchical matrix that separates and privileges the masculine over the feminine. Not infrequently, behind the demystification of the myth of development and the construction of a different relationship with nature, the demand for a free, honest voice is emerging, "a voice of its own," which questions patriarchy in all its dimensions and seeks to relocate care in a central and liberating place, undeniably associated with our human condition.[31]

3.4 Post-extractivism, Transition, and Public Policies

Discussions about the alternatives to the dominant development model in Latin America are not new to the region or unique in the world. Nevertheless, the scale and vortex of the extractive projects that are massively implemented on the continent have alerted organizations, activists, and intellectuals to the need to develop feasible alternative proposals, which, while taking into account existing exemplary models (witness cases, local and regional economies, experience of indigenous communities), are raised at a broader scale at national, regional, and global levels.

In this regard, since 2010, the contributions of the Latin American Group of Alternatives to Development (*Grupo Latinoamericano de Alternativas al Desarrollo*) can be cited.[32] In several countries of Latin America, there are already debates on the alternatives to neo-extractivism, which propose to

---

[31] There are different currents within ecofeminism, which include differentialist or identity feminism, which naturalizes the relationship between women and nature, and even constructivist ecofeminism, which conceives of nature as a historical-social construction, linked to the sexual division of labor. In Latin America, there is an important presence of popular and communitarian feminisms of a spiritualist nature that retain certain elements of the essentialist perspective, "but without demonizing the male" (Puleo, 2011) and, above all, highlight the identification with the territory and the defense of life cycles.

[32] The group, created in 2010, is promoted by the Rosa Luxemburg Foundation of Germany and addresses the issues of neo-extractivism and alternatives to it. Latin American researchers and activists and some Europeans (Alberto Acosta, Mirian Lang, Edgardo Lander, Horacio Machado, Tatiana Roa Avendaño, Esperanza Martinez, Emiliano Terán Mantovani, Pabo Bertinat, Ulrich Brand, and the author of this Element, among others are part of it). The books produced by the group have been translated into various languages.

elaborate transition hypotheses from a matrix of multidimensional intervention scenarios (Lang and Mokrani, 2013). Thus, the challenge is to conceive and establish an exit agenda for neo-extractivism and determine a passage toward post-extractivism. This implies thinking about transitional scenarios from two levels of action: the first, that of a set of public policies that act on a macro-social and global level, rather than at a small scale or at a sectoral level. The second, intervention on a local and regional scale, is aimed at detecting, valuing, enhancing, and multiplying the existing models of alter-development.

One of the most interesting and exhaustive proposals has been prepared by the Latin American Center for Social Ecology (*Centro Latino Americano de Ecología Social*, known as CLAES), under the direction of the acclaimed Uruguayan researcher Eduardo Gudynas, who states that the transition requires a set of public policies that allow us to think differently about the linkage between environmental issues and social issues. This perspective considers that a set of "alternatives" within conventional development would be insufficient compared to neo-extractivism, with which it is necessary to elaborate on "alternatives to development" in terms of a super strong sustainability model.[33] On the other hand, the need to move toward a post-extraction strategy is linked to the characteristics of a "predatory extractivism": social and environmental impacts linked to the large scale of the undertakings; high level of conflict linked to them; limited economic benefits, (re)privatization of the economy, territorial fragmentation, and distortions of the productive apparatus; the fact that many sectors depend on resources that will soon be exhausted and that the expansion of exploitation borders entails serious social and environmental risks; finally, current climate change, which imposes severe restrictions, for example, on hydrocarbon exploitation (Gudynas, 2013). The proposal emphasizes that such a discussion must be addressed in regional terms and in a strategic aspect, in the order of what the indigenous peoples have called "Good Living" or *Buen Vivir*.

In terms of public policies, one of the most problematic elements is the opposition that is to be established between social debt and environmental debt, between social and economic reform and ecological-environmental reform. This is one of the challenges and, at the same time, one of the keys to

---

[33] For Gudynas (2009), a weak conception of sustainability is one that gives a strong weight to technical instruments, with the idea of reducing environmental impacts to conserve nature to promote economic growth (ecological modernization). A strong conception of sustainability warns us that nature cannot be reduced to mere capital and underlines the importance of preserving critical natural environments by depriving them of the mercantile substrate. Finally, super strong sustainability deepens even more on the second of these positions, since it includes other valuations of nature (cultural, religious, and aesthetic), which may be even more important than economic ones. This conception breaks openly with the development-growth relationship.

deactivating a state-owned discourse and practice and converting them into a proposal that considers, among other things, a selectivity oriented toward harmony between socioeconomic reform and environmental reform. Given this, extractivist progressivism tends to affirm that this is the only way capable of generating foreign exchange, which is then reoriented to the redistribution of income and internal consumption, or to activities with a greater content of added value. This discourse, whose scope is limited and should be analyzed on a case-by-case basis, seeks to redress the social question (redistribution) to the environmental issue, while tending to overlook a series of complex and fundamental discussions that strategically connect the triple issues of upholding development, environment, and democracy.

Thus, thinking about the transition requires a set of public policies that would imply a balance between the environmental issue (limits to production, ostentatious consumption thresholds) and the social issue (poverty threshold and redistribution of wealth). In a preliminary phase, it is necessary "to move swiftly from a "predatory extractivism" to a "sensible extractivism," understood as one in which each country's social and environmental laws are fully complied with, under effective and rigorous controls, and where the impacts are internalised" (Gudynas, 2013: 175). The transition places the accent on strategic planning and on the control of natural assets by the State, reducing export dependence. The second phase should focus on essential extractive activities, that is, those undertakings that aim to cover national and regional needs, in pursuit of improving the quality of life of the people. Within the framework of a steadfast sustainability, it considers methods to limit poverty and maintain zero extinctions. In this way, it is not that a post-extraction option would imply not exploiting natural assets; rather, it would seek to reorient production to regional needs (at a Latin American level), which would entail reconstructing the perspective of what is understood by regional integration and the relationship established with the different sectors of the economy.

Perhaps one of the most complex challenges is to think about the transition in terms of the energy paradigm. As Pablo Bertinat (2013: 167–170) of the Ecologist Workshop of Rosario and energy specialist points out, the impacts of the current energy model are extensive, ranging from the direct relationship between production and consumption of electrical energy and climate change (emissions of greenhouse gases) to the impact of large infrastructure works (on territories, on populations, on biodiversity) on inequality in the appropriation of energy (the residential sector consumes only 15 percent of the energy in Latin America; the poorest pay a greater proportion of their income for energy than the rich sectors), and the absence of citizen participation, among other issues. The environmental and social damages of the current model require thinking about alternatives and energy transition models. On the other hand, it is necessary to answer more elementary questions: for example, produce energy for what and for whom? Energy appears as a subsidiary of the extractive model and this is far from having been reversed by progressive governments. In Argentina, only three mining megaprojects consume the energy equivalent to that granted by Atucha I (nuclear central); a single aluminum company like Aluar consumes as much gas as Argentina imported from Bolivia; the mining company La Alumbrera consumes more energy than the entire province of Catamarca, and, finally, the company Barrick – in Pascua Lama – will waste almost 1,000 million liters of hydrocarbons during its entire extractive process (Svampa and Viale, 2014).

Likewise, the post-extractivism hypothesis emphasizes the need to investigate at local and regional levels the successful experiences of alternative development. To reverse the logic of infinite growth, it is necessary to explore and move toward other forms of social organization, based on reciprocity and redistribution, which place important limitations on the logic of the market. In Latin America, numerous contributions come from the social and solidarity economy, whose social subjects of reference are the most excluded sectors (women, indigenous people, young people, workers, peasants), whose sense of human work is to produce usable value, or a means of living. There is, thus, a plurality of experiences of self-organization and self-management of the popular sectors linked to agro-ecology and social economy and the self-control of the production process, non-alienated forms of work, and others linked to the reproduction of social life and the creation of new forms of community. Even in a country as involved with *sojizado* (monoculture of soja) as Argentina, networks of municipalities and communities have been created that promote agro-ecology, proposing healthy food without agro-toxins, with lower costs and lower profitability, which employ more workers. A new agro-ecological framework is emerging, an archipelago of experiences that grows apart from the great soybean continent that today appears as the dominant model.

Conclusion

Nearing the End of the Progressive Cycle

At the beginning of the new century, in several countries of the region, the emergence of different progressive governments generated great political expectations among the citizens. In the heat of the consensus of the commodities, progressivism was becoming a kind of lingua franca, this is, a common language, which ordered and hierarchized the different political experiences, establishing a kind of gradation, from those more radical (the Bolivarian axis illustrated by Venezuela, Bolivia, and Ecuador) to the most moderate (Brazil, Argentina, Uruguay, among others). As has been explained in this Element, the consolidation of a progressive political hegemony was linked to the boom of the international prices of raw materials and, therefore, of the expansion of neo-extractivism.

In terms of the political cycle, progressivism was interpellated from different sectors. Within the contested space, the confrontation between different political narratives became more acute, not only in the context of the struggles against neo-extractivism and the growing criminalization of socio-environmental struggles but also as a result of political and socioeconomic limitations and inadequacies of Latin American progressivism. Thus, the socio-environmental resistances and the emergence of a new contested narrative were one result of this new context. The expansion of the border of rights (collective, territorial, environmental) found a limit in the increasing expansion of the borders of exploitation of capital, in search of goods, lands, and territories, which eroded the emancipatory narratives that had raised strong expectations, especially in countries such as Bolivia and Ecuador.

Even so, it is important to take into account the gradations and nuances of each national context. In countries such as Brazil and Chile, the eco-territorial turn, as a community key, appears associated with a set of voices belonging to the scattered and locally encapsulated groups that occupy the periphery (indigenous peoples, peasants, assemblies of small and medium localities), whereas in Bolivia and Ecuador, Theseis narratives demonstrate the convergence between indigenous protagonists and environmental organizations. In other countries, such as Argentina, a large number of socio-environmental conflicts were acquiring visibility throughout the Kirchner governments (2003–2015). They would become much more visible in the heat of the crisis, due mainly to mining.

The truth is that toward the end of the cycle (2015–2016), the split between progressives and leftists became more clearly pronounced. In some cases – such as the PT (Workers Party), in Brazil – it could even be said, as Massimo Modonesi points out, to be a "genetic mutation" (transformations); in others, we could view the evolution toward more traditional models of domination, based on a certain political tradition (high-intensity populisms, Svampa, 2016); in short, both cases apply a "conservative modernization."

On the other hand, outwardly, the progressives (populist or transformation-alist) accentuated the ideological struggle with different power groups, especially with the mainstream media. However, despite the rhetoric of war, the Latin American populisms of the twenty-first century installed a scheme similar to the populism of the twentieth century, associated with the figure of the "social pact" interclass: on the one hand, they questioned neoliberalism; on the other, they carried out the pact with the big investors. Even so, or precisely because of that, they soon found themselves immersed in a strong political-ideological confrontation with sectors of the right, connected with the mainstream media. Early political polarization processes enabled the most spurious route of the parliamentary coup, as was the case of the expulsion of Zelaya in Honduras (2009); the rapid dismissal of Fernando Lugo in Paraguay (2012); and by 2016, the impeachment of the president of Brazil, Dilma Roussef, aggravated later by the imprisonment of former president Lula da Silva (2018). Such processes accelerated the return to an openly conservative scenario in these countries. Toward the end of the cycle, right-wing critics were even more blunt: progressivisms were simply characterized as "irresponsible populisms,"[34] guilty of having squandered the period of economic boom of commodities and simply reduced to a matrix of corruption, facing scandals such as "Lava Jato" in Brazil and Odebrecht. The aim of Lava Jato is to ascertain the extent of a money laundering scheme, estimated by the Regional Superintendent of the Federal Police of Parana State in 2015 at R\$6.4–42.8 billion (US\$2–13 billion), largely through the embezzlement of funds. At least eleven other countries, mostly in Latin America, were involved, and the Brazilian company Odebrecht was deeply implicated.

The end of the cycle confronted the Latin American economies again with the crude phenomenon of inequality. Recall that the first work on inequality, based on the Gini coefficient, indicated for the period 2002–2010 a reduction of inequality in several Latin American countries. However, in more recent years, several authors have begun to qualify such statements, arguing that the available data only measured short periods and did not allow a long-term view. On the other hand, the decrease in income inequality was tied to an increase in wages, but not to a reform of the tax system, which became more complex, opaque, and above all regressive (Salama, 2015). Research inspired by the

---

[34] The concept of "populism" has a long history and a negative political charge. In Latin America, it appears associated with nationalist and/or progressive governments, unlike what happened in Europe and the United States. Certainly, the populisms of both the mid-twentieth century and the twenty-first century were progressive, with limitations and deficits, which explains why they have generated great discomfort in the left sectors. One main characteristic of progressive populisms is their ambivalence: on the one hand, they contain democratic elements of incorporation of popular social majorities; on the other hand, they deploy authoritarian elements linked to the concentration of power in the leader, to the process of fetishization of the State, to the closure of channels of pluralism. However, there is a reading from sectors on the right that tends to simplify this ambivalence typical of populisms, especially from the political/media spectrum, to reduce them to waste, corruption, and demagogy. I argue that this type of reading is partial and incomplete. See Svampa, 2016.

studies of Thomas Piketty concentrated on super-rich sectors, which take the tax declarations of the richest socioeconomic layers of the population, and showed that 1 percent of the population in countries like Argentina, Chile, and Colombia appropriates between the 25 and 30 percent of wealth (Kessler, 2016: 26).

Finally, the reduction in poverty recorded in Latin America did not translate into a reduction in inequalities. The reforms did not touch the economic interests of the elites. As Stefan Peters points out, neo-extractivism became a condition for the successful consolidation of progressive governments, but at the same time it was one of the major obstacles to the achievement of deep and structural reforms in the region (2016: 22). In 2013, the tax on the richest sectors reached 3.5 percent of the total tax collection, while the value-added tax (VAT) rose by one-third, to 36 percent, and in many countries, it became the main source of tax revenue (Burchardt, 2016: 69).

The closure of the progressive cycle does not mean the end of progressive governments. Uruguay and Bolivia continue in this way; Ecuador is torn between the progressive mutation and a transition to the right; it is to be determined what will occur in Mexico, after the triumph of Andres Lopez Obrador (2018). The fact is that we are witnessing the end of progressivism as a lingua franca, beyond governmental continuity and even developments that can be observed. And this scenario of decline confronts us with a harsh reality: within the left, the outlook is critical. The selective progressivism of the Latin American governments ended up opening deep wounds within the controversial space, difficult to heal, as the case of Ecuador shows, where sectors of the CONAIE (National Confederation of the Indigenous of Ecuador), which previously identified with the left, voted for the candidate of the right in the balloting of the presidential elections in 2017.

Where there was alternation in power, continuities are realized, but also strong ruptures with respect to the progressive cycle. The end of the progressive cycle and the transition to the right that occurred in countries like Brazil and Argentina implied not only continuities with respect to neo-extractivism but also a greater deepening, illustrated by the flexibility of the already existing environmental controls as well as the hardening of the contexts of criminalization and the increased murdering of environmental activists, in disputes over land and access to natural assets. These transformations take place in a political scenario that shows a strengthened right, which exhibits an increasingly aggressive neo-entrepreneurial and anti-progressive rhetoric, especially after the overwhelming victory of Jair Bolsonaro in Brazil, which increasingly places in a quagmire respect for the freedoms and basic rights of the most vulnerable populations.

Despite this, there is a line of accumulation in the field of socio-environmental disputes, with even global resonances. Beyond the asymmetries, the Latin

American region has asserted a broader assessment rhetoric of the territory, alternative methods of building a link with nature, alternative forms of organization of social life, and alternative narratives surrounding the earth. Such narratives aim to recreate a relational paradigm based on reciprocity, complementarity, and care and point to other modes of appropriation and dialogues of knowledge. Different political-ideological matrices nourish this speech – anti-capitalist, ecologist, and indigenous; feminist and anti-patriarchal perspectives – which are a result of the heterogeneous world of the subaltern social classes.

In short, in Latin America, the critique of neo-extractivism and the debate regarding transition are influenced by alternative ways of inhabiting the territory. Additionally, such proposals postulate the democratization of the debates, since these decisions cannot be restricted to the elites, whether they be economic, political, or technical. They imply, therefore, the activation and expansion of participatory mechanisms and direct democracy. These processes of (re) territorialization are accompanied by an innovative political-environmental narrative associated with BV and the rights of nature (*Derechos de la Naturaleza*, common goods (*Bienes Comunes*), and the ethics of care (*Etica del Cuidado)*, whose key is both the defense of the commons and the recreation of another relational link with nature – a crucial social and environmental rational.

References

Acosta, A. (2009). *La maldición de la abundancia*, Quito: Ediciones Abya Yala. (2013). "Extractivism and neo-extractivism: two sides of the same curse," pp. 61–87, in *Permanent Group of Alternative to Development*, M. Lang and D. Mokrani (eds.), *Beyond Development. Alternative Visions from Latin America*, Luxembourg, Netherlands: Transnational Institute Luxembourg – Rosa Foundation.

Acosta, A. & Brandt, U. (2017). *Salidas del laberinto capitalista. Decrecimiento y Postextractivismo*, Madrid: Icaria.

Acselard, H. (ed.) (2004). *Conflitos ambientais no Brasil*, D. Relume (ed.), Rio de Janeiro:Fundaçao Heinrich Böll.

Antonelli, M. (2011). "Megaminería, desterritorialización del Estado y biopolítica," in Astrolabio, nro 7. https://revistas.unc.edu.ar/index.php/astrolabio/article/viewFile/592/3171

Bebbington, A. (2009). "The new extraction: rewriting the political ecology of the Andes?" *NACLA Report on the Americas*, *42*(5), 12–20.

Bellamy Foster, J. (2000). *La Ecología de Marx – Materialismo y Naturaleza*, El Viejo Topo (ed.), Carlos Martín and Carmen González (trans.).

Bertinat, P. (2013). "Un nuevo modelo energético para la construcción del buenvivir", en Grupo Permanente de Trabajo sobre Alternativas al Desarrollo (2013). *Alternativas a capitalismo/colonialismo del siglo XXI*, Quito, Rosa Luxemburg Foundation.

Bertinat, P., D´Elia, E., Ochandio, R., Observatorio Petrolero Sur, Svampa, M., & Viale, E. (2014). *20 mitos y realidades del fracking*, Buenos Aires: Editorial El Colectivo.

Bolados, P. (2016). "Cartografías del extractivismo minero en el desierto de Atacama-Norte de Chile," pp. 91–110, in Zhour, A., Bolados, P., & Castro, E. (eds.), *Mineranaçao Na America Do Sul. Neoextrtrativismo y lutas territoriais*, Brazil: Annabluma Editora.

Bolados, P. & Sánchez Cuevas, M. (2017). "Una ecología política feminista en construcción: El caso de las 'Mujeres de zonas de sacrificio en resistencia,' Región de Valparaíso, Chile." *Psicoperspectivas*, *16*(2), 33–42. DOI 10.5027/psicoperspectivas-vol16-issue2-fulltext-977

Bonneuil, C., & Fressoz, J. B. (2013). *L´événement antrhopocène. La terre, l´histoire et nous*, Paris: Seuil.

Bottaro, L. & Sola Alvarez, M. (2016). "Escalas, actores y conflictos: etapas de la movilización en respuesta al avance de la megaminería en Argentina," pp. 111–30, in Zhour, A., Bolados, P., & Castro, E. (eds.), *Mineranaçao Na America Do Sul. Neoextrtrativismo y lutas territoriais*, Brazil: Annabluma Editora

Burchardt, H. J. (2016). "El neo-extractivismo en el siglo XXI. Qué podemos aprender del ciclo de desarrollo más reciente en América Latina," pp. 55–89, in Hans-Jurgen, B., Domínguez, R., Larrea, C., & Peters, S. (eds.), *Nada dura para siempre. Neoextractivismo después del boom de las materias primas*, Quito: Ediciones Abya-Yala.

Carpio, S. (2017). "Integración energética sudamericana: entre la realidad, perspectivas e incertidumbres," pp. 91–13, in *Discursos y realidades. Matriz energética, políticas e integración. Plataforma Energética*, Bolivia: CEDLA.

CEPAL, (2013a). *Recursos Naturales en UNASUR. Situación y tendencias para una agenda de desarrollo regional*, Santiago de Chile: CEPAL.

(2013b). *Los bonos en la mira: aporte y carga para las mujeres*, Observatorio de Igualdad de Género de América Latina y el Caribe. Informe Anual 2013. www.cepal.org/publicaciones/xml/7/49307/2012–1042_OIG-ISSN _WEB.pdf

(2015). *Anuario Estadístico de América Latina y el Caribe*, Santiago de Chile: CEPAL.

Chicaiza, G. (2014). *Mineras chinas en Ecuador: Nueva dependencia*. Quito: Agencia ecologista de información Tegantai.

Composto, C. & Navarro, M. L. (2011), *Territorios en disputa: entre el despojo y las resistencias. La megaminería en México*, "Entender la descomposición, vislumbrar las posibilidades," México. https://horizontes comunitarios.files.wordpress.com/2014/02/territorios.pdf

Coper-acción, "Nuevo mapa y reporte de concesiones." http://cooperaccion .org.pe/cooperaccion-presenta-nuevas-herramientas-para-analizar-concesiones-mineras/

Coronil, F. (2002), *El Estado mágico. Naturaleza, dinero y modernidad en Venezuela*, Venezuela: Consejo de Desarrollo Científico y Humanístico de la Universidad Central de Venezuela – Nueva Sociedad.

Cortes, D. (2012) "La construcción social del Buen Vivir en Ecuador", in *Plataforma del Buen Vivir,* www.plataformabuenvivir.com/2012/03/cor tez-construccion-social-del-buen-vivir/

De Echave, J. et al. (2009). *Minería y Conflicto social*, Lima, IEP-CIPcA.

Delgado-Ramos, G. C. (2010). *Ecología Política de la minería en América Latina. Aspectos socioeconómicos, legales y ambientales de la mega minería*, Centro de Investigaciones Interdisciplinarias en Ciencias y Humanidades, México: UNAM.

(2016). "Configuraciones del territorio: despojo, transiciones y alternativas," pp. 51–70, in Navarro, M. & Fini, D. (eds.), *Despojo capitalista y luchas comunitarias en defensa de la vida en México, Claves desde la Ecología Política*, México: Ed. Universidad Benemérita de Puebla.

Descola, P. (2005). *Más allá de naturaleza y cultura*, Buenos Aires: Amorrortu.

Díaz Polanco, H. (2008). "La insoportable levedad de la autonomía." La experiencia mexicana. pp. 245–273, In Gutierrez Chong, N. (ed.), *Estados y Autonomías en democracias contemporáneas*, México: Plaza y Valdés.

Documento de las organizaciones de derechos humanos para el Foro Permanente para los pueblos indígenas. (2010). *Situación de los derechos humanos de los pueblos indígenas en Bolivia, 2010*, La Paz, Bolivia.

Escobar, A. (2005). "El post-desarrollo como concepto y práctica social," pp. 17–31 in Mato, D. (ed.), *Políticas de Economía, ambiente y sociedad en tiempos de globalización*, Caracas: Facultad de Ciencias Económicas y Sociales, Universidad Central de Venezuela.

(2011). "Cultura y diferencia. La ontología política del campo de cultura y desarrollo," *Revista de investigación en Cultura y Desarrollo*. http:// biblioteca.hegoa.ehu.es/system/ebooks/19420/original/Cultura_y_ diferencia.pdf?1366975231

(2014). *Sentipensar con la tierra. Nueve lecturas sobre desarrollo, territorio y diferencia*, Bogotá, Colombia: Ediciones Unaula.

Esteva, G. (2007). "Commons: más allá de los conceptos de bien, derecho humano y propiedad." Interview with Gustavo Esteva by Anne Becker. Conferencia Internacional sobre Ciudadanía y Comunes, México, December.

Falleti, T. G. & Riofrancos, T. N. (2018). Endogenous participation: strengthening prior consultation in extractive economies. *World Politics*, *70*(1), 86–121.

Feliz, M. (2012), Proyecto sin clase: crítica al neoestructuralismo como fundamento del neodesarrollismo," pp. 13–44, in Feliz, M. et al. (eds.), *Más allá del individuo. Clases sociales, transformaciones económicas y políticas estatales en la Argentina contemporánea*, Buenos Aires: Editorial El Colectivo.

FIDH (Federación Internacional de Derechos Humanos). (2015). "Criminalización de Defensores de Derechos humanos en el contexto de fenómenos industriales. Un fenómeno regional en América Latina." www .fidh.org/IMG/pdf/criminalisationobsangocto2015bassdef.pdf

Fondo de Acción Urgente – América Latina (2017). *Extractivismo en América Latina y su impacto en la vida de las mujeres*, Colombia: FAU-AL.

Fontaine, G. (2003). "Enfoques conceptuales y metodológicos para una sociología de los conflictos ambientales, escrito a propósito del petróleo y los grupos étnicos en la región amazónica," pp. 503–33. http://library .fes.de/pdf-files/bueros/kolumbien/01993/12.pdf

Gandarillas, M. (2013). "Extractivismo y derechos laborales. Dilemas del caso boliviano." www.cedib.org/wp-content/uploads/2013/07/empleo_hegoa_ gandarillas.pdf

(2014). "Bolivia: la década dorada del extractivismo," pp. 67–103 in *Extractivismo: nuevos contextos de dominación y resistencias*, Cochabamba: CEDIB.

García Linera, A. (2012). *Geopolítica de la Amazonia*, Bolivia: Vicepresidencia del Estado Plurinacional.

Gargallo Celentani, F. (2015). *Feminismos desde Abya Yala. Ideas y proposiciones de las Mujeres de 607 pueblos en nuestra América*, Bogotá, Ediciones Desde abajo.

Gilligan, C. (2015). *La ética del cuidado*, Barcelona, Cuadernos de la Fundació Víctor Grífols i Lucas. www.secpal.com/ percent5CDocumentos percent5CBlog percent5Ccuaderno30.pdf

Global Witness (2014) www.theguardian.com/environment/ng-interactive/ 2017/jul/13/the-defenders-tracker y www.jornada.unam.mx/ultimas/ 2018/02/02/asesinan-acerca-de-200-defensores-del-medio-ambiente-en- 2017-global-witness-5318.html

Goffman, E. (1974). *Frame analysis: An essay on the organization of experience*. Cambridge, MA: Harvard University Press.

Gudynas, E. (2009a). "La ecología política del giro biocéntrico en la nueva Constitución del Ecuador," *Revista de Estudios Sociales*, 32, 34–47.

(2009b). "Diez tesis urgentes sobre el nuevo extractivismo," AAVV, *Extractivismo, Política y Sociedad*, Quito: CAAP, CLAES.

(2013). "Transitions to post-extractivism: directions, options, areas of action," pp. 165–88, Permanent Group of Alternative to Development, Lang, M. and Mokrani, D. (eds.), *Beyond Development. Alternative Visions from Latin America*, Netherlands: Transnational Institute- Rosa Luxembourg Foundation.

(2015). *Extractivismos. Ecología, economía y política de un modo de entender el desarrollo y la naturaleza*, Bolivia: CLAES-CEDIB.

Haesbert, R (2011), El mito de la desterritorialización: del "fin de los territórios" a la multiterritorialidad, México: Siglo Veintiuno.

Harvey, D. (2003). *The new imperialism*. New York: Oxford University Press, pp. 209–13.

Hoetmer, R., Castro, M., Daza, M., & de Echave, J. (2013). *Minería y Movimientos sociales en el Perú. Instrumentos y propuestas para la defensa de la vida, el agua y los territorios*, Lima: Cooper-acción, PDGT.

Holbraad, M. & Pedersen, M. A. (2017). *The ontological turn. An anthropological exposition*, Cambridge: Cambridge University Press.

Houtart, F. (2011). *De los bienes comunes al bien común de la humanidad*, Quito: Fundación rosa Luxemburgo.

Kessler, G. (ed.). (2016). *La sociedad Argentina hoy. Radiografía de una nueva estructura*, Buenos Aires: Siglo XXI-OSDE.

Korol, C. (ed.). (2016). *Feminismos populares. Pedagogías y Políticas*, Buenos Aires: América Libre-El Colectivo.

Kothari, A., Salleh, A., Escobar, A., Demaria, F., and Alberto, A. (eds.). (2018). *Pluriverse: A post-development dictionary*, Delhi: Authors Up Front/ Tulika/Columbia University Press.

Laboratorio de Paz.(2016). "Estado reconoce en CIDH que no ha realizado estudio de impacto ambiental para Arco Minero," June 6, 2016. www.laboratoriosde paz.org/estado-reconoce-en-cidh-que-no-ha-realizado-estudio-de-impacto-ambiental-para-arco-minero

Lander, E. (2013), "Tensiones/contradicciones en torno al extractivismo en los procesos de cambio: Bolivia, Ecuador y Venezuela," in AAVV, *Promesas en su laberinto. Cambios y continuidades en los gobiernos progresistas de América Latina*, Quito: CEDLA.

Lang and D. Mokrani (eds.), (2013) *Beyond Development: Alternative Visions from Latin America*, Permanent Group of Alternative to Development. The Netherlands, Transnational Institute- Rosa Luxembourg Foundation

Leff, E. (2004). "La ecología política en América Latina: un campo de construcción," pp. 23–41, in Alimonda, H., *Los tormentos de la materia,. Aportes para una ecología política latinoamericana*, Buenos Aires: Ediciones de Clacso.

Machado Aráoz, H. (2012). *Naturaleza mineral. Una ecología política del colonialismo moderno*, Tesis para optar por el título de Doctor de Ciencias Humanas, Facultad de Humanidades, Universidad Nacional de Catamarca, Argentina.

(2013). "Crisis ecológica, conflictos socioambientales y orden neocolonial. Las paradojas de NuestrAmérica en las fronteras del extractivismo." *Revista Brasileira de Estudos Latino-Americanos* REBELA, 3(1), Outubro de 2013. Escola de Administração, Universidade Federal do Rio Grande do

Sul, Porto Alegre, pp. 118–155. ISSN 2237-339X. http://rebela
.edugraf.ufsc.br/index.php/pc/article/view/137

(2014). *Potosí, el origen*, Buenos Aires: Mardulce.

Machado Araoz, H., Svampa, M. et al., Colectivo Voces de Alerta (2011), *-15 mitos y*, Svampa, M. et al. Colectivo Voces de Alerta (2011). *-15 mitos y realidades sobre la minería transnacional en Argentina*, Buenos Aires: Editorial El Colectivo-Ediciones Herramienta.

Machado, D. & Zibechi, R. (2016), *Cambiar el mundo desde arriba. Los límites del progresismo*, Bogotá: Ediciones Desde Abajo.

Martinez Allier, J. (2004). *El ecologismo de los pobres. Conflictos ambientales y lenguajes de valoración*; Barcelona: Icaria Antrazo; FLACSO ECOLOGÍA.

(2015). "El triunfo del posextractivismo en 2015." February 28, 2015. *Sinpermiso* www.sinpermiso.info/textos/index.php?id=7778

Meyer, D. & Gamson, W. (1999). "Marcos interpretativos de la oportunidad política," in McAdam, D. McCarthy, J. and Zald, M. (eds.), *Movimientos Sociales, perspectivas comparadas: oportunidades políticas, estructuras de movilización y marcos interpretativos culturales*, Madrid: Ediciones Istmo.

Modonesi, M. (2016). "Subalternización y revolución pasiva" in *El principio antagonista. Marxismo y acción política*, México: Itaca-UNAM

Moore, J. W. (2011). Ecology, capital, and the nature of our times: accumulation & crisis in the capitalist world-ecology. *Journal of World-Systems Research*, *17*(1), 107–46.

Murcia, D. & Puyana, A. M. (2016). *Mujeres indígenas y conflictos socio-ambientales*, Bogotá, Programa Fortalecimiento de Organizaciones Indígenas en América Latina Deutsche Gesellschaft für Internationale Zusammenarbeit (GIZ) GmbH. www.infoindigena.org/images/ Publicaciones_generales/Genero/Mujeres-Indgenas-y-conflictos-socio-ambientales-f.compressed.pdf

Navarro, M. L. (2015). *Luchas por lo común. Antagonismo social contra el despojo capitalista de los bienes naturales en México*, México: Ediciones Bajo Tierra.

Observatorio de igualdad de género de América Latina y el Caribe (OIG) —— (2013). *Los bonos en la mira: aporte y carga para las mujeres*, Observatorio de Igualdad de Género de América Latina y el Caribe. Informe Anual 2013. www.segib.org/wp-content/uploads/Losbonosenla_Informe_AnualOIG_ 2013.pdf

Observatorio Petrolero Sur (OPSUR) (2018), "La CIDH recibió con preocupación denuncias sobre el fracking en América", www.opsur.org

.ar/blog/2018/10/04/la-cidh-recibio-con-preocupacion-denuncias-sobre-el-fracking-en-america/

O´Connor, J. (2001) *Causas naturales. Ensayo de marxismo ecológico*, Buenos Aires, siglo XXI, disponible. http://theomai.unq.edu.ar/Conflictos_sociales/OConnor_2da_contradiccion.pdf

OCMAL. (2011). *Cuando tiemblan los derechos. Extractivismo y Criminalización en América Latina*, Quito: Ocmal, Acción Ecológica.

Oxfam Internacional. (2014). *Las mujeres rurales de América Latina son luchadoras, no criminale.* www.oxfam.org/es/crece-peru-mexico-el-salvador-guatemala-bolivia/las-mujeres-rurales-de-america-latina-son-luchadoras

(2016). *Unearthed, land, power and inequality in Latin America.* www.oxfam.org/sites/www.oxfam.org/files/file_attachments/bp-land-power-inequality-latin-america-301116-en.pdf

Padilla, C. (2012). "Minería y conflictos en América Latina" pp. 37–58, in Toro, C., Fierro Morales, J., Coronado, S., & Avendaño, T. (eds.), Bogotá: Censat-Universidad Nacional de Colombia.

Palacios Paez, M., Pinto, V., & Hoetmer, R. (2008). *Minería Transnacional, Comunidades y las Luchas por el Territorio en el Perú: El caso de Conacami*, Lima: Coper.Accion & Conacami.

Paredes, J. (2008), *Hilando fino. Desde el feminismo comunitario*. http://mujeresdelmundobabel.org/files/2013/11/Julieta-Paredes-Hilando-Fino-desde-el-Fem-Comunitario.pdf

Permanent Group of Alternative to Development. (2013). Lang, M. & D. Mokrani, *Beyond development. Alternative visions from Latin America*, Netherlands: Transnational Institute- Rosa Luxembourg Foundation. www.tni.org/files/download/beyonddevelopment_complete.pdf

Peters, S. (2016). "Fin del ciclo: el neo-extractivismo en Suramérica frente a la caída de los precios de las materias primas. Un análisis desde una perspectiva de la teoría rentista," pp. 21–54, in Burchardt, H. J. et al. *Nada dura para siempre. Neoextractivismo después del boom de las materias primas*, Quito: Ediciones Abya-Yala.

Porto Gonçalves, C. 2001. *Geografías, Movimientos Sociales. Nuevas Territorialidades y Sustentabilidad.* México: Siglo xxi.

Porto Gonçalves, C. 2017. "Amazonia, Amazonias. Tensiones territoriales actuales." *Nueva Sociedad*, 272: 150–159.

Puleo, A. (2011). *Ecofeminismo para otro mundo posible.* www.mujeresenred.net/spip.php?article1921

Quijano, A. (2014), "Buen Vivir. Entre el Desarrollo y la descolonialidad del poder," pp. 19–34 in Quijano, A. (ed.), *Descolonialidad y Bien Vivir. Un nuevo debate en América Latina*, Lima: Universidad Ricardo Palma, https://mega.nz/#!BZsWCRSB!ykPizlEmpuUzZPFwxA9aQ1Hv6hQeNCu HGqsnY9z9ILc

Roa Avendaño, T. & Navas, L. M. (eds.). (2014). *Extractivismo, conflictos y resistencias*, Bogotá: Censat-Agua Viva, Amigos de la Tierra de Colombia.

Roa Avendaño, T., Roa García, M. C., Toloza Chaparro, J., & Camacho, M. (2017), *Como el agua y el aceite. Conflictos socioambientales por la extracción petrolera*, Bogota: Censat-Agua Viva.

Roa Avendaño, T. & Scandizzo, H. (2017). "Qué entendemos por energía extrema," in *Extremas. Nuevas fronteras del extractivismo energético en Latinoamérica*. Oilwatch Latinoamérica. Buenos Aires: Opsur.

Rodríguez Garavito, C. (2012), *Etnicidad.gov: los recursos naturales, los pueblos indígenas y el derecho a la consulta previa en los campos sociales minados*, Bogotá, Dejusticia, Cap.1. El derecho en los campos minados. 8–24. Documento en pdf.

Rodríguez Garavito, C. (ed.). (2016). *Extractivismo versus derechos humanos. Crónicas de los nuevos campos minados en el Sur Global*, Buenos Aires: Siglo XXI.

Romero, C. & Ruiz, F. (2018) "Dinámica de la minería a pequeña escala como sistema emergente," pp. 87–144, in Gabbert, K. & Martínez, A. (eds.), *Venezuela desde adentro. Ocho investigaciones para un debate necesario*, Quito: Fundación. Rosa Luxemburgo.

Sacher, W. (2016). "Segunda contradicción del capitalismo y megaminería. Reflexiones teóricas y empíricas a partir del caso argentino." Flacso-Ecuador, PhD thesis.

(2017. *Ofensiva megaminera china en los Andes Acumulación por desposesión en el Ecuador de la 'Revolución Ciudadana*, Quito: Abya Yala.

Sacher, W. & Acosta, A. (2012), *La minería a gran escala en Ecuador*. Quito: Abya Yala-Universidad Politécnica Salesiana.

Sack, Robert (1986). *Human territoriality: Its Theory and History*, Cambridge, Cambridge University Press.

Salama, P. (2011). "China-Brasil: industrialización y 'desindustrialización temprana'" *Open Journal Sistem*, Universidad Nacional de Colombia. www.revistas.unal.edu.co/index.php/ceconomia/article/view/35841/39710

(2015). "¿Se redujo la desigualdad en América Latina? Notas sobre una ilusión," *Nueva sociedad*, Buenos Aires, July-August. http://nuso.org

(2017). "Reprimarización sin industrialización. Una crisis estructura en Brasil." Revista Herramientas. www.herramienta.com.ar/articulo.php? id=2567

Santos, M. (2005). "O retorno do territorio". *Reforma agraria y lucha por la tierra en América Latina, territorios y movimientos sociales* vi, núm. 16.

Schuldt, J. & Acosta, A. (2009). "Petróleo, rentismo y subdesarrollo. ¿Una maldición sin solución?" in AAVV, *Extractivismo, política y sociedad*, Quito: Ediciones del CAPP y CLAES.

Slipak, A. (2013). De qué hablamos cuando hablamos de reprimarización? Un aporte al debate sobre la discusión del modelo de desarrollo, VI Jornadas de Economía Crítica. https://www.academia.edu/7188437/ _De_qu%C3%A9_hablamos_cuando_hablamos_de_reprimarizaci% C3%B3n_Un_aporte_al_debate_sobre_la_discusi%C3% B3n_del_modelo_de_desarrollo

Shiva, V (2005), La mirada ecofeminista. Tres textos, in *sin Permiso*, www .sinpermiso.info/textos/la-mirada-ecofeminista-tres-textos

Sola Álvarez, M., & Bottaro, L. (2013). "La expansión del extractivismo y los conflictos socioambientales en torno a la megaminería a cielo abierto en Argentina." *Revista latinoamericana PACARINA de Ciencias Sociales y Humanidades* 4: 89–100.

Solon, P. (2016). https://fundacionsolon.org/?s=El+Bala.

Svampa, M. (2008). *Cambio de Época. Movimientos sociales y poder políti*co. Buenos Aires: Siglo XXI-Clacso.

(2013), "Resource extractivism and alternatives: Latin American perspectives on development," pp. 117–44 in Permanent Group of Alternative to Development, Lang, M. & Mokrani, D. (eds.), *Beyond development. Alternative visions from Latin America*, Netherlands: Transnational Institute- Rosa Luxembourg Foundation.

(ed.). (2014). *Actores, conflictos y modelos de desarrollo en la Argentina contemporánea*, Buenos Aires: Ediciones de la UNGS, pp. 9–19.

(2015). "Commodities consensus: Neoextractivism and enclosure of the commons in Latin America." *South Atlantic Quarterly, 114*(1), 65–82.

(2016). *Debates Latinoamericanos. Indianismo, Desarrollo, Dependencia y Populismo*, Buenos Aires: Edhasa.

(2017). *Del cambio de época al fin de ciclo. Gobiernos Progresistas, extractivismo y movimientos sociales*, Buenos Aires: Edhasa.

(2018a). *Chacra 51. Regreso a la Patagonia en los tiempos del fracking*, Buenos Aires: Sudamericana.

(2018b). *Las fronteras del neo-extractivismo en América Latina*, México: CALAS-Universidad de Guadalajara.

(2018c). "Latin America development: Perspectives and debates," pp. 13–32 in Falleti, T. & Parrado, E. (eds.), *America since the left turn*. Philadelphia, PA: University of Pennsylvania Press.

Svampa, M. & Slipak, A. (2018). "Amérique latine entre vieilles et nouvelles dépendances: le rôle de la Chine dans la dispute (inter) hégémonique," pp. 153–66 in *Herodote*, Géopolitique de l'Amérique Latine, 171, Quatrième trimestre 2018.

Svampa, M. & Viale, E. (2014). *Maldesarrollo. La Argentina del extractivismo y el despojo*, Buenos Aires: Editorial Katz.

Terán Mantovani, E. (2016). "Las nuevas fronteras de las *commodities* en Venezuela: extractivismo, crisis histórica y disputas territoriales," *Ciencia Política, 11*(21), 251–85.

Tola, F. (2016). "El 'giro ontológico' y la relación naturaleza/cultura. Reflexiones desde el Gran Chaco, *Apuntes de Investigación del CECYP* 27: 128–39.

Toledo, V. (2013). "El metabolismo social: una nueva teoría socio-ecológica," *Relaciones* 136: 41–71.

(2016). "Salir del capitalismo! La revolución agroecológica y la economía social y solidaria en América Latina," pp. 143–158, in Coraggio, J. L. (ed.), *Economía social y solidaria en movimiento*, Buenos Aires: Ediciones UNGS.

Unceta Satrustegui, K. (2015). *Más allá del crecimiento. Debates sobre Desarrollo y Posdesarrollo*, Buenos Aires: Mardulce.

Vidal, J. (2017). "Why is Latin America is so obsessed with mega-dams?" *The Guardian*, May 27. www.theguardian.com/global-development-professionals -network/2017/may/23/why-latin-america-obsessed-mega-dams

Villegas, P. N. (2014). "Notas sobre movimientos sociales y gobiernos progresistas," pp. 9–66, in *Extractivismo: nuevos contextos de dominación y resistencias*, Cochabamba: CEDIB.

Viveiros De Castro, E. (2008). *La mirada del jaguar. Introducción al perspectivismo amerindio (entrevistas)*, "El cascabel del Chaman es un acelerador de partículas," pp.9–34, Buenos Aires: Editorial Tinta Limón.

Zavaletta Mercado, R. (2009). *Lo nacional-popular en Bolivia*, La Paz: Plural.

Zhouri, A., Bolados, P. & Castro, E. (2016). *Mineranaçao Na America Do Sul. Neoextrativismo y lutas territoriais*, Brasil: Annabluma Editora.

Cambridge Elements ≡

Elements in Politics and Society in Latin America

Maria Victoria Murillo
Columbia University

Maria Victoria Murillo is Professor of Political Science and International Affairs at Columbia University. She is the author of *Political Competition, Partisanship, and Policymaking in the Reform of Latin American Public Utilities* (Cambridge, 2009). She is also editor of *Carreras Magisteriales, Desempeño Educativo y Sindicatos de Maestros en América Latina* (2003), and co-editor of *Argentine Democracy: The Politics of Institutional Weakness* (2005). She has published in edited volumes as well as in the *American Journal of Political Science, World Politics, Comparative Political Studies* among others.

Juan Pablo Luna
The Pontifical Catholic University of Chile

Juan Pablo Luna is Professor in the Department of Political Science at The Pontifical Catholic University of Chile. He is the author of *Segmented Representation. Political Party Strategies in Unequal Democracies* and has co-authored *Latin American Party Systems* (Cambridge, 2010). His work on political representation, state capacity, and organized crime has appeared in *Comparative Political Studies, Revista de Ciencia Política*, the *Journal of Latin American Studies, Latin American Politics and Society, Studies in Comparative International Development* among others.

Tulia G. Falleti
University of Pennsylvania

Tulia G. Falleti is the Class of 1965 Term Associate Professor of Political Science, Director of the Latin American and Latino Studies Program, and Senior Fellow of the Leonard Davis Institute for Health Economics at the University of Pennsylvania. She is the author of the award-winning *Decentralization and Subnational Politics in Latin America* (Cambridge, 2010). She is co-editor of *The Oxford Handbook of Historical Institutionalism*, among other edited books. Her articles have appeared in many edited volumes and journals such as the *American Political Science Review* and *Comparative Political Studies*.

Andrew Schrank
Brown University

Andrew Schrank is the Olive C. Watson Professor of Sociology and International & Public Affairs at Brown University. His articles on business, labor, and the state in Latin America have appeared in the *American Journal of Sociology, Comparative Politics, Comparative Political Studies, Latin American Politics & Society, Social Forces*, and *World Development*, among other journals, and his co-authored book, *Root-Cause Regulation: Labor Inspection in Europe and the Americas*, will be out soon.

About the Series

Latin American politics and society are at a crossroads, simultaneously confronting serious challenges and remarkable opportunities that are likely to be shaped by formal institutions and informal practices alike. The new Politics and Society in Latin America Cambridge Elements series will offer multidisciplinary and methodologically pluralist contributions on the most important topics and problems confronted by the region.

Cambridge Elements ≡

Elements in Politics and Society in Latin America

Elements in the Series

Understanding Institutional Weakness: Power and Design in Latin American Institutions
Daniel M. Brinks, Steven Levitsky, and Maria Victoria Murillo

A full series listing is available at: www.cambridge.org/PSLT

CPSIA information can be obtained
at www.ICGtesting.com
Printed in the USA
LVHW031922211019
634872LV00014B/444/P